Charm & Passion

Vol. 1

Edited by Jasmine Redd
Designed by Skyler Warren

Copyright © 2016 by Sasha Dixon and Jasmine Redd

All rights reserved. No part of this publication may be reproduced, distributed, or transmitted in any form or by any means, including photocopying, recording, or other electronic or mechanical methods, without the prior written permission of the publisher, except in the case of brief quotations embodied in critical reviews and certain other noncommercial uses permitted by copyright law. For permission requests, write to the publisher, addressed "Attention: Permissions Coordinator," at the email address below.

unafraidtotell@gmail.com

ISBN:0692824790

This book is dedicated to my mother and best friend who first challenged me to write spoken word poetry, my stepfather and dad who always shows me the power of love and kindness, my only brother and two sisters who have always believed in my ability to compose and perform, and to every individual I have encountered who has made an impact in my life.
~Charm

This book is dedicated to my loving grandparents Dorthy Allen and Harvey Lee Allen. Thank you for adopting and supporting me and all of my dreams. You have truly encouraged me to set my expectations above the standard bar. I love you with all my heart and know God has divinely blessed me with each of you.
~Passion

Table of Contents

All of my Charm by Jasmine Redd

Cellphones or Cellblocks?	1
Untamed Intention	2
Musical Mind	3
First	4
Moments in Motion	5
Art	6
Better	7
Copy Paste	8
Dead on Arrival	9
Injected Control	11
Poetry	12
Press Play	13
Remedy	14
Second Wave	15
State	16
Temple	17
Corruption	18
Things We Should Have Said	19
Word	20
Choose	21
Design	24
Dream	25
The Same	26
Remains	27
Last Supper	28
Snake	29
Strength	30
Ahead	32
Father and Daughter	33
Cheers	34
Happiness Rendered	35
JMS James	36
Love Lost, Love Gained	37
Ready or Not	39
Selling the Dream	41
The Other Woman	42
Understand	43
Webster's Dictionary	44
I Am	45
Give	46
Reason	47
Cheater	48
Right	49
Power	50
Alive	51
Just Friends	52

Mountains and Hills	53
Empty	55
Beautiful Struggle	57
Beautiful Surprise	58

All of my Passion by Sasha Dixon

Dream or Reality	60
Danced to the Beat	62
Started To	64
Feeling a Death	66
Expressed Drive	67
Face of a Dove	69
Change	71
You're Frozen	73
Outside the Window	75
The Man with the Plan	77
A Hold	78
Mind Heated	80
Speak the Truth	82
She Rose	83
My Blackbird	85
I Never Felt the Need to	86
9 to 5	88
You Decide	90
When the Time Comes	92
What Could I Say?	94
Lord Save the King	95
Sitting at the Park	97
I'm Not in Love with You Anymore	98
The Force	100
I Don't Want to Hear	102
Let the Wickedness	104
We Journeyed into the Wilderness	106
You Asked Me	108
With My Soul	110
I Don't Want Another Dream	112
Your Loyalty Does Not Lie with Me	114
I'm in a Constant Battle	116
Tittle Trail Mix	118
They Did Me Wrong	120
Keep Smiling	122
I Shared	124
Just Be Glad	127
Our Lips and Ears	129
If You Love Him	131
Too Late	133
I Didn't Make the Deadline	135
No One Will	137
You're Moving	139
The Blind Can See Your Envy	141
No Words	143

First Look and Find 145
Who Can See the Wind? 147
So He Said 148
Pray 150
Touch the Stars 151

Cell phones or Cellblocks?

I walk on this earth, but I choose to be trapped in my cell
I actually paid for my own imprisonment,
Confined to the invisible walls that the screen displays
This *is* my world.
Held to my face, perfectly encased
I'd feel naked should it ever be misplaced
I embrace, my false sense of reality
Cut corners with devices, instilled with pseudo-sagacity
Brag about my right to have individuality
But we're afraid to be different in all actuality
Our sense of connection is conveniently shattering
Cell phones are now a part of convivial gatherings
Head down.
Our eyes that used to love the natural world are now obsessed with digital
Not remembering that they once gazed upon all beauty in the physical
And the freedom to speak is now hindered by tweets, likes, hearts and other trivial substitutions
That bind the essence of in-person dialogue and create more confusion
Technological evolution is a form of execution to the value of true communication
Acting in automation, we've abandoned imaginations in place of a few applications
Indeed, the cell phone is the cellblock of multiple generations
Screens are the new playgrounds, text is the new voice
Confined to this small device, all by choice.

Untamed Intention

Sometimes, it seems like I can't stand up to the bully in my mind
It reminds me, of my weaknesses and never forgets to mention the last time I added to my unfulfilled promises
It harnesses, all the fears that keep me from truly experiencing the best parts of life
It hates change and wants me to stay in my depressed manner
Saying success doesn't really matter,
The golden years were in high school and half way through college as if that will be the ultimate peak of my life
And the rest of my years will be spent reminiscing on when I had better self-discipline, self-control, motivation towards goals and a true understanding of my own…power.
It wants me to busy myself with hobbies of dancing, dating, playing house, but never really getting out of my head
My head that, gets excited about responsibility then finds an excuse as to why I don't have the capability to finish the task
I ask, my mind for permission to try something different, but it never fully commits
Because it's out of its comfort zone and we know that's what leads to change, transformation and enlightenment
So it stagnates my environment,
Covers my desires, blacks out my goals to be somebody, heal diseases, help the world by never channeling my focus on starting with me
It scatters my energy, it's the ultimate mastermind of never discovering me
Like a great girlfriend, devoting my broken pieces to a foundation, hoping they'll fuse into a stronghold,
But expressing love to another before loving yourself is like, driving with a blindfold
It just…doesn't…really…work.
And in that mindset, everyone gets hurt.
Even though I feel like I can't stand up to the bully in my mind,
I have to remember they are just thoughts that haven't manifested in real time
And their only train to my reality is my sheer belief in their duality
That these negative thoughts are protecting me,
But really they're infecting me,
Possessing me with their poisonous approaches to life
At what point do I end this tyrannical strife?
I must start with myself, this innate ability to give
Only when I control my untamed intention to live.

Musical Mind

Every time the oldies play, I can't help but to find
Music taking me on an experience, courting my mind
Knocking on the door of my imagination
Asking for my hand in choreographic creation
Leading me into sight-seeing rhythmic patterns
With bedazzled costumes and lyrical dancers
Eighth notes step carefully next to staccatos
While whole notes sit cozily next to legatos
Staff in my hand, I place them into position
Each having a role and a proposed intention
In my intuitive ear, I now hear and listen
To Ro James seductively asking for my permission
Which is cute, but he's a little outside of his reach
To Mr. White who commands me to practice what I preach
Who understands the power of his baritone speech
Who bears such creativity you just can't teach
Each time I turn on the radio, I just keep my eyes closed
And hear the heartbeats of each artist through the song they composed
I envision a ribbon in the sky that only Stevie and I know
Overjoyed by the possibility of a new love to grow
But Luther takes me out, to a dinner so pristine
Before Michael dips me on the floor, he's a dancing machine
Later I talk with Aretha about demanding some respect
By these chain of fools who always want me to forget
I mean, I feel good with James, so nice I couldn't even see
That Marvin tried to remind me things ain't what they used to be
I confess to Tina that despite the code this crumbling world lives by
My love for meaningful music will remain river deep, mountain high.
This medley of music has my creativity in bloom
Injected with inspiration, having not even left the room
And every time the oldies play, I can't help but to find
Another note induced into my musical mind.

First

I couldn't finish writing him a love poem
Well, because I needed to express my love to someone else first
Really, not "someone" but "the only one."
The only one who would sacrifice His life for mine
The only one, who in total darkness, can still shine
My catalyst because He is the only one who causes change in my life
Who removes, only to give
And who never reneges
But I only mind Him before I eat and well,
That's about it.
Amen.
Let's be honest, I'm not proud, but I don't pray like I should
I remember when we conversed each morning before the sun stood
But now, I sleep in
Because that seems to be more important than meaningful time with the only one who will forgive, teach and guide me
I'd be, so confused if I missed even one day without Him beside me
And so far I've missed 893, I mean I'm not counting…
But I realize without Him, I'm incessantly doubting
Yet when I look at the man who looks lovingly into my eyes
Who wipes my tears as I cry
I know it can only be a sign that "the only one" is nearby
See, I know how I feel and when emotions are peaked,
I speak, but my words come out empty
I'm too busy trying to be lovely instead of loving the only one worthy of being loved first
God, why do you even quench my thirst?
I know the love I give You could never compare
To the sacrifice of Your life so I could be spared
I feel You in my atmosphere, always vying for my attention
Dear Lord, I'm so sorry that I never fully listened
To Your proverbial wisdom, I stand shocked at what You've given me
This incredible gift of love that has always grown and lived in me
And as he and I hold hands, I tell this loving man that my focus is on you
That he may not pursue me until I have been made new
Where You and I will share love seamlessly, talk frequently each day
God, I am hungry for Your shift and yearning for Your change
Today, I express my love to You.

Moments in Motion

It seems we only understand the importance of time when we're hooked up to machines
Intersecting life and death is when we begin to understand our dreams,
Realizing we were too busy to do anything we wanted or should have done,
Like all of the victories that should have been won,
The apologies that should have been spoken,
Relationships that should have never been broken,
Kindness that should have been shared,
An understanding ear that should have been spared,
Laughter that should have been increased,
Anger that should have been released,
Lips that should have been kissed,
Sights that should have not been missed,
I mean, what really matters?
Money, fame, cars, power?
When the sweetness of life has suddenly gone sour,
Will you really ponder possessions in your final hour?
It's time we start living with purpose and devotion
Our lives are movies played of moments in motion
Witnessed by all we encounter and those we hold dear
What will they see when your movie airs in so many years?
Scenes of when you rushed home from obligations, feeling your time stretched thin?
Rushed to bed, setting the alarm to start all over again?
Will they see when you rushed to work, weaving through traffic?
Rushed your way through a life that always remained static?
You are better than any moment that faced you as tragic
To make beauty of ruin yields impeccable magic
Live a colorful life, scenes seamlessly woven like fabric
Marked as unforgettable and revered as a classic.

Art

Cultivate your art, the definition of your existence
Stands on premise of your constant persistence
Despite the interference, that nearly killed your spark
You are the only one who can leave your mark
Dark times will come,
So be who you thought you couldn't be
Because you let your passion
Speak louder than your pity
Than your pride, than your fear
When you let go of the tears,
When you begin to see the world, when its message is clear
All that will be left is you, standing here.
A work of art,
Shaped and shifted, but never broken apart
The start of a crack reveals stories untold
But will never be forgotten as the years unfold
Bold curves hold pleasure, deep cuts hold pain
Your beauty holds my gaze and I can see every stain
But every color was a witness to life once lived
As were the two-toned spots that time couldn't forgive
And while others pass by,
Unaware of your battles,
I can tell by the scars
You never hid in the shadows,
Your journey is mysterious, yet the art that was produced
Feels familiar and draws me closer each time I gaze upon you,
Not wishing to leave your powerful presence
Because you left an impression with your undeniable essence
Each morning I rise, I envision your artistic bloom,
But now I have the privilege to watch you blossom in my room
Your cultivated art leaves me forever changed
And what you did for me, for someone else I shall do the same.

Better

You say you want things to be better
But how do you really feel?
You say it's going to take time
To trust and to heal
But you push yourself away
And cry of how you are alone
You want so much in return
And yet must cast the first stone
I'm an advocator of change
But can't really help with self-pity
I won't assist you in playing the victim
Or making the ugly seem pretty
I won't beg you to like me
I can't change how you perceive me
But you better believe I'll be there
If you should ever need me
You say you want things to be better
But how do you really feel?
The way you look at me sometimes
If looks could really kill
I'd be shot and chopped up
Maybe exploding into flames
Not sure what I've done wrong this time
Or who's to really blame
But I can't walk on eggshells
I tread heavily with passion
So you can either be my ally
Or try to become my assassin
I support your position
Whichever route you choose
Just understand there's always a predictable way
To win and to lose
You say you want things to be better
But action says it louder
So if you do what is most difficult
It will unlock your power
We cannot change the past,
But we have today to begin
If we want things to be better
We must start from within.

Copy Paste

She says she doesn't really have the time, to be original
She writes, but never by hand, her phrases are digital
She only caters to the outside, all efforts plainly physical
Neglecting the cultivation that is needed for the mental
The next generation won't even know what it's like to create
To be original, to stand out, to initiate instead of wait,
Won't know how to format the layout of life, orientation, page breaks
Because that generation will only know duplication, copy paste
The true genius in making music, has now gone to waste
For, the flavor it used to carry doesn't have the same taste
My palate has become bitter by the constant chatter and chitter
As their uninventive rhymes leave my mouth filled with litter
When did we start suppressing and stop being our own emitter?
Exuding intuitive influence,
Composing our own history instead of a melancholic continuance
I mean constructing your own experience, not replicating what is popular
In fact, sometimes I admit my speech a little uncopular
We don't always use am, is, are, was, were
Like the American Vernacular and some cultures prefer
But that, is a part of being unequivocally authentic
We feel no need to copy the Nazi's use of eugenics
I want to remain beautifully different, the mark of my life is all I have
And all I have to do is decide I don't want to trod a beaten path
We can't perform math on a miracle, but I know if we act with haste,
We can stint the process of bringing in generation copy paste.

Dead on Arrival

I put in an order to the source of the ultimate giver
Seven days later, I read the status as delivered
It was rendered to my door, so thankful was I to receive it
But after gazing at its contents, I simply couldn't believe it.
This was not what I asked for, I requested a miracle
Hadn't I fulfilled what was asked? Hadn't my faith been spiritual?
I needed this, to awaken my soul,
A matter of death or survival,
But for me, it did nothing at all
My order was dead on arrival,
Nor did it resemble the attributes I succinctly described
What I thought could calm my mind, I now wish to hide
What I thought could be my guide appears to have already died
Lord, please tell me why my request was denied?
DOA, in my stressful state, tell me how am I to cope?
When the only answer provided is to channel my hope,
But being hopeful is painful so I'm dying to believe
That of all you have created, you haven't forgotten about me.
I can't afford to miss this change based on my man-made calculation
For if I do, I'll remain in a state of total devastation
Left to burn in a self-made perpetual conflagration
I demand answers, there's a reason why this came to my location
Excuse my intonation, most High, it seems I just can't clear my head
I can't stop thinking, I asked for peace to be delivered and have a notebook instead
Lord, did you hear me? I have no need for objects at this time
I'm in desperation, my sense of sanity is on the line
And soon to cross over, but you reminded me you crossed over life, death, and resurrection
For all, including me, to have salvation and protection
That, you hear even my thoughts I have not spoken in tongue
That you are the only link between changing what can be done and undone
You ask, "child, why do you run? Why do you ask for what I've already given?
Do you not remember what I did for Elisha when he needed a child risen?"
Suddenly, I was struck with a blow of curiousity
Searching the appendix, table of contents, glossary
In my biblical mind filled with every philosophy
As the Lord favorably decreased my childish animosity
You see, Elisha prays to bring the boy to life and firmly understands
He must connect with him, mouth to mouth, eyes to eyes, hands to hands,
But life is not granted until he stretches on him, until he expands
Sneezing several times, the boy is revived and now able to withstand.
The notebook I viewed as a dead object actually has the power to revive me
By removing the dead thoughts and rotting neuropathways deep inside of me
And as God made Elisha able to bring life to the lifeless

I know he can make me capable of overcoming this crisis
Lord, your timing is priceless, I now understand my gateway to peace
I accept this tool of internal renewal as a method of my release
Ultimate giver, you have abundantly delivered
And to think, I almost selected return to sender...

Injected Control

On August 15, 2016
A notice was published by the CDC
Proposed Rulemaking was the title I saw
To amend federal public health law
They want travelers, with a cold or a cough
Suspected of being ill
To be taken and isolated for days,
Held against their will
I'm tired of being ruled by unruly persons
Without morals, but with titles
Who will then have the right to tell me if I've become viral
Who, over my God-given body, wants to have the power
To detain and quarantine me for 72 hours
Against my will until they feel I'm not the threat the suspected
Or until I agree to be vaccinated, voluntarily injected
I haven't felt protected since our food stopped being simple
It's now modified and artificial, deeply affecting our temples
The government doesn't care about truly protecting you and me
The government only truly cares about two trite things:
Money and power.
And it's their power that gives the CDC freedom to publish such a notice
I ponder the motives behind why this organization actually wrote this
We are trained to believe that other entities can carry our concerns with their voice,
But not speaking for ourselves is accepting our own demise by choice
See, because we give them permission, to speak on our behalf
But they don't have the same purpose and passion that we have
To graph visually, the CDC
Analyzed the effectiveness of the flu vaccine
Between 2005 and 2015
And at best, these were the results that were seen:
Less than 50% effective more than half of the time,
Being forced to take any vaccination, should be a crime
This is not the first time we've dealt with a cold,
We're not starting at ground zero,
But we have a government that induces panic
Just to pretend to be the hero
So I will not sit silently, quietly, nod my head in affirmation
I will not, blindly agree and accept any more deceit from another corrupt organization
I will choose to vaccinate myself with only hope and possibility
Instead of chemical atrocities that hold me in captivity
I will speak against injustice, even if I touch only one soul
Even if I challenge one mind, I would have achieved my goal:
To spread the knowledge of a force called injected control.

Poetry

Part of being a poet is not being afraid of disagreeable moments
Being a poet is not about being right or politically correct,
It is simply expression in its truest form.
I do not come on stage to be applauded or admired
I come to express what life means in my eyes,
Through the breath that moves between my lips
And it is ok, if we are not on the same page
Because if I tried to be, I wouldn't know what my voice would sound like,
So concerned about mimicking yours
I don't stand before you to be dissected, categorized by color, appearance, diction,
Being a poet is not about biting your tongue when there's friction,
But it is about being vulnerable,
Dressed only by each word that drops from my mouth,
Clothed by phrases, clauses and causatives
I wear it outside of me because there is no more room left inside of me
This poetry, frames my language,
Sentences displayed as remarkable art
My unequivocal method of leaving my mark
You will remember the first time a poet speaks to you
And everybody has a poet inside, waiting to be pursued
But we are all so shy, avoiding the watching eyes of the "who"
See, being a poet has nothing to do with them, but everything to do with you
So choose,
To speak,
Poetry.

Press Play

I hope you enjoyed watching my life,
But the movie I debuted wasn't even my truth
I had deleted scenes and an extended version
That never made it to the booth
You viewed only, smiles and laughter
It was all I wanted you to see
Because I didn't think you'd continue watching
If you saw all of me,
But even when the credits rolled, you still wouldn't leave...
You knew there was something missing,
The storyline just wasn't practical
After my charade, I showed the real movie,
No theatrical
Only factual representation and unedited scenes
Would be displayed for you to see on an HD screen
I pressed play, opening you to my vulnerabilities
Introducing you to my strongholds and minor insecurities
My subtle fears transformed into fragility
But never controlled my immovability
I pressed play, the projector flashed, the inner workings reeled
27 hours, one hour for every year of my life, plainly revealed
The wall, on which my life was played, was my solid black reflector
And when the film was completed, he rose to his feet and wanted to meet the Director.
Me.
Whom he had just seen inside out
Face to face, we held gaze, but no words came out
Then he said, "In your next movie, I propose *we* be the stars
I plan to never leave your side, for I love everything you are"
Tears in my eyes, head in my hands, this man was my equal
27 and beyond, the next movie debuting, stay tuned for the sequel.

Remedy

At, what point did we start believing we couldn't take care of ourselves?
That, only doctors could, diagnose?
That, only drugs could, heal our bodies?
At, what point did we start believing treating a symptom was better than, going to the source?
That, a drug causing graver side effects than, the original problem was actually worth the risk?
That, over-the-counter relief was better than, a permanent cure?
At, what point did we start believing we could treat cancer with chemotherapy
With, this mustard gas used historically to kill our enemies?
When did we start believing in a quick-fix remedy?
And when will we start believing in our natural identity?
Void of pharmaceutical breakthroughs and toxicity?
When will we start standing against chemical extremity?
Maybe when all of our loved ones die from diseases that could have been treated with diet
Maybe when we realize the hospitals don't cure and band together in a riot
Maybe when we become fed up with being specimens for their experiments
Maybe when we understand chemicals will never lead us to lifelong merriment
Life holds no guarantee, but healthy food has become my go-to remedy
And pharmaceutical companies that claim to heal have become my darkest enemy
We need to stop relying on antibiotics and chemical pills on shelves
And re-learn how to master our bodies by taking care of ourselves.
You, have the remedy.

Second Wave

Here I sit with my glass of red wine
Overthinking which words will create my next line
We live together, his pillow next to mine,
But we think separately in this space and time
Could I spend a lifetime with him by my side?
Are we really willing to endure this ride?
I must revive myself.
I have lied to myself, believing I can give 100 when I only give myself 10
I don't want to pretend,
Pretend that I'm satisfied when I can feel a divide
Between what we say we want and how we really feel inside
We didn't want to abide by the rules
So we cohabitated before marriage,
Choosing to be economical,
Cutting the corners of courting,
Ultimately selling ourselves short on what we want to achieve
But neither of us, are willing to leave…
And yet something still makes me feel incomplete.
Perhaps our initial approach was unbecoming to our vision
Maybe we thought we heard intuition, but hadn't keenly listened
However, now I am in tune and I possess no confusion
We can't expect a real experience by only adding substitutions
Lord, take us on a journey extending past where we've been
More in love with your guidance, help us begin again.

State

What state do you live in?
I used to say Texas
But now, I live in the state of truth
Its walls are my shelter, its revelations are my food
Truth opens its doors for me to reside
Because it is my home, I have no need to hide
Nor do I have pride, I embrace all of its residents
Because they understand that being true to yourself, takes precedence
The state of truth has happiness as its capital city
The scenery is too pretty to wallow in self-pity
Although the state of pain is one of its neighboring borders
Many people from that state seem to always cross over
Because happiness is contagious and is encouraged to be spread
It continues to revive you when pain pronounces you dead
We always discuss the physical states, but rarely the emotional
Most of it lives in our head and our actions become notional,
But I'm devotional to my truth, and I encourage you to begin
To evaluate the emotional state you reside in.

Temple

I must be careful with what I place inside
Only the best can be sacrificed at your altar
I give you my promise of purity,
To let nothing infect your walls
Not even when night falls and temptation calls...

I must be cautious with what I place inside,
Choosing wisely by knowing what labels hide
I give you my undivided attention, my vow of value
As what touches my lips will only come from quality instead of convenience
I no longer have obedience to the fast-food allegiance...

My temple is too important to be tainted with impurities
Causing disorders and leading to disease
I choose a philosophy that is virtuously simple:
I must be careful with what is placed in my temple.

Corruption

"Get the F on the sidewalk" was the first communication
That has only fueled more division amongst the cultures in this nation
He was killed on location, minutes from his destination
With two-sided accusations, Michael, this poem is in dedication,
To you.
Two days away from college, fresh out of high school
Gone before your time, a victim of misrule
Because this world is indecent, merciless and cruel
CNN says it's a he-said, she-said case,
But I know better than to believe that when talking about race
Tensions are high, the justice system is rigged
Protesters hold up their hands as the teenager once did
We are amid injustice, that could have been you or me
Running for our lives in the middle of the street
Only to be murdered in cold blood, I retell
Truman Capote knows that story all too well
How do you live in a system where the laws are unjust?
It only intensifies this longevous history of distrust
Darren's identity was confidential because death threats began,
But how is it that he was protected even though he killed an innocent black man?
Corruption.
Corruption.
Corruption has tainted some minds to believe
That taking a life has the consequence of a paid administrative leave
He has lost nothing, while the Brown family grieves
Reliving the daunting memories of that murderous eve.
Years have passed, but nothing has changed
The underlying issues still remain the same
We are at war and we always were
Be ready for battle, for anything could occur
This corruption still stirs...

Things We Should Have Said

I love you
Even though you appear
Unlovable in your own eyes

Unlovable in your own eyes
You appear so beautiful in mine
I promise to always give you space and time
I promise

I promise
Our time will be quality
And you will always be a priority
I'll show you,
You can trust in me

You can trust in me
Not just with your heart,
But with every endeavor you want to start
I want to create with you

I want to create with you
Not just go by the rules
And if you put your gem in my possession,
I know we can produce more jewels
You shine so brightly

You shine so brightly
Darkness can't even penetrate your light
I will fight for you

I will fight for you
You are worth every tear and upheaval
And though the world may seem evil
Your love is my comfort
I will walk with you

I will walk with you
Even when you want to be alone
I'll never leave your side
You are the only person I want on this ride
No swap-outs or cop-outs
You are everything I'm about

You are everything I'm about
With my undivided attention
I am present to this gift we've created
The syncopated beating only gets stronger
The longer we are together
My heart won't stop until it knows you forever
In all the things you've wanted to say

My heart won't stop until it knows you forever

I never knew you felt this way
Things we should have said.

Things we should have said.

Word

You are your word.
They say you are what you eat
I say you are what you speak
The thoughts you think become manifestations in speech
Crafted in mind, projected into reality
Unique in its expression of individuality
These words, they are contracts that bind yourself to your desires
You could either prove to be a liar or accomplish what you aspire
Your word is your copyright, your patent, your brand
And lets other know what you expect, where you stand
You are what you speak and of that, which can be heard
More than letters side by side, you are your word.

Choose

With infinite choices, the world diverts our attention
From the certainty of Jesus, filling us with apprehension
And even though we are made in his image, his literal extension
We are instantly uncomfortable when God's name is even mentioned
We are distracted and often detract from the mercy that he gives
Highly impacted and hijacked from the lives that we live
Sinful by nature, our desire displaces us
Unaware of the law we abide by until His grace faces us
See in the beginning, it was perfect
Nothing hidden beneath the surface
That is, until the serpent
Placed doubt within God's servant
Eve was her name, she was taken out of Adam
Amidst a paradise of a garden that no one here can fathom
It began here, the Devil's cunning ways
God saw Eve as pure, the Devil saw her as prey
Twisting the truth, ultimately leading her astray
Making her question God with the punctuation that we do 'til this day.
To love God and never trust him is nothing more than spiritual fraud
Let your praise on the service be something more than a façade
With all of our advancements, don't you think it's rather odd
That our iniquities continue to separate us from God?
No, we have choices.
And I always thought I was from a different time
The content of my spirit doesn't fit here and I find
That the world has misplaced us and we can't find ourselves
Yet we always find ourselves of Facebook
Or tweeting a friend about the latest trend instead of the Heavenly book
E-nook won't really allow me to feel its pages
I just scroll with my finger, these digital cages
Trap my creativity, I touch the screen
But there is no connection between it and me.
Technology is an addiction that takes over our lives
Strung out on Facebook waiting for our next like
Fascinated with whose following us or who we can follow
Being a leader nowadays sure is hard to swallow
I don't want my hope to sound hollow, but we're becoming empty without substance
Filling our temples with chemicals, not worried about the Day of Judgment
But if you pay attention to what God is teaching you
You will understand that your earthly leaders are misleading you
My people. At least that's what Isaiah says.
It's time we make a choice.
See, spiritually I'm rich, but monetarily I'm poor
And if my faith is not enduring, I will not endure
So I'll take it. I won't remake it like my generation
These masonic iconoclastic idols we listen to on these stations
Strip away our values for the purpose of building their nation

And we let them by refusing a Godly transformation
We would rather be blind sheep led by the wicked elite
Than to trust Jesus who died for us, humbling ourselves at his feet
We are not made to be analogous to each other, but to do as he speaks
And when I think of how Jesus struggled, it displays my struggle as weak
But he examined me, tried my heart and gave caution to the wind
And though I want to say he has found nothing evil and my mouth has not sinned
I would be a liar before the testimony of my body
Who falls victim to my hobbies
Through this glass is my copy
I look at you. Dressed in my worst choice
Accessorized with glum feelings and a non-existent voice
In my mirror, your reflection is staring
I want to say I acknowledge you, but don't mistake it for caring
The act of a physical exchange has never been more despairing
Has never felt more brutal across my skin tearing
But as I face you, I realize I've placed you off your throne
Allowed entry into your temple for fear of being alone
I say the fault is my own
Hoped for an experience that would add to my wisdom
But a moment of satisfaction altered the path to my kingdom
Instead of experiencing freedom,
You suffered.
You. Suffered.
You suffered because of my unwillingness to pay attention
Because I paid desire to take me to another dimension
But it only left me in debt and each time I owed you apologies
What you needed and what I wanted were of two separate ideologies
And now finally,
Defendant, my desires
Plaintiff, my body.
On trial with two sides of myself on the run
Who will I become when it is all said and done?
Spiritually in-tune or a woman of the wild?
Along the way somehow I forgot that I was still his child.
His wildflower that grows in the middle of Death Valley watered by the rain of circumstance.
This wildflower is accepting, never rebellious, never doubting
Allows its protective coating to be removed for the purpose of sprouting
But how many of us cease to shed our coating and instead become complacent
Never exchanging old ways and habits for an upgraded replacement?
I should be guilty, but I'm forgiven, sin washed clean
I am full of fault, but there is only one who can judge me
I'll share with you and be honest, I won't stand here and pretend I have wings
Because the truth heals, even though the first realization stings.
You can try to hide your sins behind your possessions as a shield
But everything you have done, are doing or will do will soon be revealed.

So will you discipline your attention or play the victim of the diversion?
Are you content with who you are or do you want a better version?
The decision is yours, pay no mind to other views
Jesus chose to save mankind, what will you choose?

Design

They tell me who I am based on what they see
A daughter, a professional, a young lady
I may be a dancer, and even a poet,
But I'm also a designer, crafter of moments
Being a designer is not just a profession
You have this ability in your possession
To design your life, to create your path
What you desire is everything you can have
It's not just a skill some people have acquired
There's no special wire, you just have to be inspired
To visualize your dream is to build the foundation
The base on which your wishes come into formation
Design without limit, have infinite rooms
That represent ideas awaiting their bloom
Don't be discouraged if locked doors lack shine
Each door is always opened at the most fitting time
Some things I can't control, but I have free will to use
So I can choose to see a win for me even when I think I'll lose
They always tell me who I am based on what they see
But I'm most interested in who I believe myself to be.

Dream

I've been stuck at 211 degrees
Remaining hot, but not at boil
See the only way to create more steam
Is if to your dreams you stay loyal
I admit, I've been distracted
Unsure of the route I wish to follow
The space once filled with purpose
Now feels barren and hollow
I swallow deeply at the thought
Of remaining at this heat
It's enough to always want,
But never enough to move my feet
I drag them, but I want to run
To travel beyond this place,
But I cannot advance in life
Unless I look myself in the face
In the eyes, see the goal
Hear the cries of my soul
Regain my power to control
But when? Only God knows
The omniscient and omnipotent one
He feels me in this place
He tells my subconscious
Who tells my mind to just have faith
So I do as instructed, retaining my heat
For I'll soon cross over this line
And all I have desired, all I have wanted
Will deservedly be mine
I dream to be at 212 degrees
With power because I'm at boil
Because the only way to create more steam
Is if to your dreams you stay loyal.

The Same

I expect nothing from you
Except the frequent excuse
Of why you are too busy,
I will not be disappointed
When you turn a cold shoulder
After asking me to come over
I only expect you to be who you've always been,
Distant.
And I would be foolish to ever expect you to be my friend
I know you treat strangers better than you treat your kin
And that would normally make me upset
Except I don't expect anything from you,
And if I do receive contact because you're in a good mood
I will accept because my greatest regret
Would be to be like you.
To hate like you,
Love with conditions like you,
Cast anger like you,
Pretend like you,
I expect nothing from you
Except the frequent excuse
Of why your unhappiness is everyone else's fault
A story that apparently only you have bought
You assault yourself each day, but want someone else to be arrested
You want others to make you happy but for them, you have no time invested
I've tried to understand you and I used to reprimand you
But now I don't demand you to change
I just expect nothing from you except the frequent excuse
Of why you'll always be the same.

Remains

I played with fire, spontaneously it came
The fire erupted, for the glow of the flame
Engulfed me, left my eternal soul maimed
Because I encountered him, I'll never be the same.

We held each other like we had known each other for years
But what is left after the heat of the moment disappears?
It seemed all I could remember was holding back tears
Losing me while loving him was one of my greatest fears

He conducted heated love like electricity
Shocking my entire body from my head to my feet
AED's were no match for his TLC
Hypnotically he paralyzed me with his ability
To love without limit, forgive without reason
Never lose ground while the external changed season
When we collided, my frost had subsided
My frozen heart melted where the flame was ignited
And my wouldn't body suddenly became would again
I found the good again, in us
Removed the doubt, increased the trust
Embraced the ice to leave us just...
Falling in love with every step, you see
I thought he was the cause of my wondering
But as he is here right in front of me
I couldn't have been more wrong in my interpreting.

To love another doesn't equate to losing yourself
If you understand your needs don't have to be shelved
I played with fire, spontaneously it came
But the fire subsided, no glow of the flame
We held each other like we had known each other for years
But what is left after the heat of the moment disappears?
The heat of the moment may not always sustain
But the love left behind will always remain.

Last Supper

I throw you away just to pick you out of the trash
Always looking back at what I can rehash
And the process is so crass, the craving so incredible
I think, maybe if I dig you out again, you will become edible
I mean, able to make me full
See, light snacks are for fools
You were meant for fuel, an object of renewal
So I place you on a platter against a frame that is white
The issue is, you never satisfy my appetite
Yet from the platter I eat and no the taste is not sweet
But I convince myself that you may be good for me
Maybe my body can't resist you if I consume you consistently
Even though this same recipe made me sick last week
But I don't want the time in preparing you to go to waste
So I say I'll learn to love you, you'll become an acquired taste.
Cognitively I question the follow through of my view
Because how often, do things work out the way we want them to
It's true, I threw you out last month but never took you to the curb
You just stayed in my bag and you were never disturbed
Until I had the urge to feed my curiosity
Became focused on the vision and never the veracity
I wondered how you would taste with ambition in your ingredients
How rich your flavor could have become had your process been expedient
I was obedient in waiting on your blossom, for your petals to rise
But the external can't flourish if the inside dies
And you, see, you were never a flower
I spent so much time masking a scent that grew to be sour
Promised to try again and again but the time was not ours
It was always in God's hands, see, we never had the power
So by the next time I shower
I will have placed you in a case, wrapped you up in tape and thrown your memories away
Hoping the next mouth you encounter will understand the complexity of a meal like yours
You were prepared to be eaten once
But I made myself sick consuming you over a period of months
Happily hunted I found you in a blaze of glory
I preyed on you but never prayed over you, which concluded our ending story:
A half-eaten ill-prepared weather-beaten never paired relational cuisine.
What looks good on the platter could fancy my appeal
But once the secrets are revealed, it hardly seems ideal
It's time to wrap this up with a double heavy duty seal
For fear of missing the preparations for my next and final meal.

Snake

Surreptitious movements
Clever turns
Vicious bites
    Awaiting in the dark
    Watching you
    Without lights
        Jealous, owning nothing
        Wanting all
        That you have
            Waiting on the moment
            That you will
            Cross its path
                Unaware of danger
                Walking blind,
                Having fun
                    But when you hear the scream
                    Then you feel
                    Total stun
                        Seeing something slither
                        On the ground
                        Where you step
                    Leaves you filled with terror
                    Of the fate
                    You'll accept
                Fear ensues your body
                What you thought
                Was your friend
            Has turned into a snake
            And the bond
            Was pretend
        Now falling to your knees
        Fatal fangs
        Pierce the skin
    Thoughts of trust remind you
    What this tie
    Should have been
Your mind wants to believe
Fellowship
In the end
    But snakes never intend
    On making
    Life-long friends
        Surviving the attack
        Makes you think
        Of each scar
            Who we appear to be
            Isn't quite
            Who we are.

Strength

He told me,
You are that very rare embracing warmth of sunshine and captivating beauty
At the start of a beautiful morning sunrise
Just after it has turned from cool to warm
A sunshine that is so very loving, comforting, vibrant and all encompassing
That you can do nothing but bask in how splendid it feels against your skin
So splendid as if the universe smiled down on you and chose to embrace you with a loving hug...

His hands moved to my hips and as poetry spilled from his lips,
He eclipsed me.
Women.
We want that man, don't we?
We want him to take care of us, love us, and protect us
But when we get him, we shout our independence and instruct him not to smother us
My mother was and still is a strong woman
Never asked for help and only really relied on herself.
My mother and best friend has educated me
On being independent, self-sufficient, and never relying on someone else to save my day,
But tell me,
What is strength?
Holding back tears?
Biting your tongue?
Hardly expressing emotion when life leaves your bloodstains on the floor?
Smeared.
I step on it with pride at the bottom of my shoe
But really it is only the illusion of strength that I portray to you
And if you were honest, you would admit that you do it too
But most of you wouldn't recognize your own reflection
Choosing to see who the world wants you to be instead of following a guided direction
Claiming to know your power, perhaps a higher endeavor
Reassuring you're in control, but the strings have never been severed
And to your surprise, you never even knew they were there.
I remember the exact moment it hit me, as if in thin air
Like 200 falling pianos from the sky
Sitting in my car, he faced me,
I, symmetrical to his stance,
He began to speak and said,
You make it hard for a man to take care of you...
What does he mean?
I was only expressing my independence
To not need him for anything that he wanted to support me with,
Didn't he appreciate my strength?
But what is strength?

And who gets to decide
If my reaction to life somehow makes me more qualified?
I learned from my parents that physical strength could be abused
Self-ambitional strength could ruin a family
And emotional strength could silence vulnerable expression
So the lesson I grasped when I met this loving man
Went against any idea I had previously held in my right hand
I demanded that strength was
Severing ties after one mistake to protect from being hurt
Choosing not to be committed to be a surreptitious flirt
Never exposing a weakness or asking for help
Leaning on no one and doing everything by myself
I held this idea to the highest degree
But after he posed his statement to me
I saw I was the woman I had spoken of previously
Wanting a man to love and take care of me, such an inspiring depiction
Yet when he arrived, I shouted my independence, such a contradiction
So sitting in my car, I faced him,
He, symmetrical to my stance,
I, began to speak and said,
Nothing quite yet
I had to collect my thoughts
Because if my response was too weak, my sense of power would be shattered
But if I came on too strong he would feel like he didn't matter
All of this cranial chatter
Left me in silence.
I grew tired of being a victim of internal conflict and violence
Spending most of my time in mind than manifesting thoughts in real time
I, looked in the rear-view's shine
Took his hand in mine
And asked one more time
What is strength?
Self-defined.

Ahead

He knew how to do what I was in school for and offered to help,
But I never took him up on his offer.
I was too afraid he would have a piece of me he didn't deserve
Could I ever forgive him for walking out on us?
For beating my mother?
For hurting my brother?
For putting himself before his family?
Could I ever allow him to be a grandfather?
To teach my kids?
His twisted sense of reality leaves me with every discomfort imaginable
His presence in my life has become simply unfathomable
The moments he missed are now rather incalculable
Using words like "father" taste bitter, unpalatable
I believe this relationship is no longer salvageable
Though, sometimes, even when my grandmother calls me every year on my birthday,
I still think maybe one day he will follow suit
I still want him to care, but part of me knows he'll always refute
Who is it that I want him to be? Should he remain a stranger?
Should he try to become someone in my life that keeps me enclosed from danger?
Should he try to work his way up from minor to major?
The only one who knows this is life's cosmic arranger
And, I'm not in control of that
All I know is that he turned his back
All I know is that his presence lacks
All I know is that image of an almost attack
Could I ever let it all go?
One thing is for certain, our connection is dead
But only God knows what lies ahead.

Father and Daughter

I need to get it out
All the nasty memories,
Bitter tears and broken eyes matched with hearts,
Get it out, pour it out of my soul
Stained with angry stares
Do I dare cross the line and tell you who you were there?
I mean, back then,
When you and Whiskey were the closest of friends
And music was the wannabe
Wanting you to sing "Making Love Between the Sheets"
But neither could make you the father you were supposed to be
The picture is not pretty and I won't apologize for its appearance
What remains is the broken glass in frame masking your disappearance
And I take the bits of fragment as they lacerate my hands
Funny, I find traces of your blood tainted on the next man
They are in debt to you, must pay for your errors
Must speak quietly because a raised voice brings terror
They must not be jealous, for it may lead to abuse
These are the lessons that your daughter has learned from you.
Besides the occasional math problem and a love of old school,
Thank you for the memories,
The images that won't soon leave me
The rolled up shirt on the neck of my brother, placed in a corner with a bright red face of confusion, hurt, and anger all combined
And I find that if I dig deeper
I hear my mother crying for hours because after 25 years
Because a divorce was requested,
Breaking up the family she poured her life into so you can focus on your own,
But all you will be left with is yourself in the end
Yet, one day you will be gone and all the hurt you caused won't matter.
So I choose to get you out of my system,
Purge you like an addiction
So that the constant replaying of memories
Can't cause any more affliction
And though you may never reach the standard you could have pursued
You are my father in blood and God says to honor you
So titles are all you and I will share,
Father and daughter.

Cheers

I would like to make a toast
To a world whose disease has yet to be diagnosed
They say I have a condition so I'll try to make the most
Of this life, in which to death I've been very close.
See, I was born dying, the world tries to murder me, so I've been living my life in dreams
Someone please free me from Eurocentric ideals, I've been held hostage by their strings
They misunderstand me, they label and brand me as an iconoclast
But why don't we wake up with a vision when we come from such a virulent past?
We've come from torture to triumph, but what happened to the voices?
Because those voices are the reason why we now have so many choices
Understand, we don't have a Charles Chestnutt to feel the marrow of tradition
To write with great ambition about changing our position
And we lack a Ralph Ellison to teach self-definition
This invisible man had identity, but he was seen as an apparition
And these children are missin' a Zora Neale Hurston mission
Their eyes were watching God but he's now far from recognition
So how do we change this condition
Tap into intuition
So that we may begin to live life of our own volition
Without one man's permission or subservient submission
We came from a time where black was opposition
Where racial unification was indeed a prohibition
But years of experience have given birth to transition
If you could just listen, our history remembers
The violence and the riots on the eve of September
The segregation of bathrooms and classrooms and genders
The movements of sacrifice, sufferance, surrender
So that their woes may not be rendered, upon this generation
So that we could have the chance to enrich our education
To compete in occupation, to envision aspiration
To experience opportunity, instead of limitation
And while we drive through life with such different navigation
We mustn't forget as we provide augmentation
So without further hesitation
I mean, this is a celebration
So I toast to another level of racial complication
It is further illustration of the strength in our creation.

Happiness Rendered

This glove is no longer a glove, this dove, no longer a dove
I now view ordinary things through a lens of love
Because of who you are, because of what you do
I don't need sex to confirm my love for you
See, love's venue is more meaningful, doused with memories
Remembering moments that make life exemplary
Inside jokes like rotisserie chicken
Laughable ideas that only you and I can mention
See I always pay attention, even when you think I don't listen
And when you say I love you, your left eye always glistens
I want you and I to move into another dimension
See, stages of life are only levels of contention
So after each dissention we'll walk through love's redemption
I don't fret over the small things, I know your intentions
Loving you this way was never really my prediction
But I think the ability to love was God's greatest invention
So I'll hold on to you, like hands hold flowers
Like government holds power
Like time holds hours
I'll, turn your problems into positive perspectives
So you can properly follow God's proposed objectives
I'll even, challenge your mind, but never your manhood
Question the tales which have been misunderstood
About love.
How do you know when your soul speaks?
Love at first sight is a popular belief
But eyes can't read what codes define you
They only reveal what brands design you
So I'm talking about L-O-V-E.
See I'm equipped with consonants so I'm only able to L-V
But I knew my soul was speaking when you answered with an O-E
So I'm not worried about the thrills that others wish to pass my way
You are essential to the appetite of what my soul craves to say
"At last, my love has come along..."
And at the end of the day when the rays of sun fade and the temptuous night tends to linger
I will lay and trace the silhouette of your face with the tip of my index finger
So I can, aim you in the center of my dreams
And drift off with you until my mind is serene
So I can understand why so long I have waited
Why your name and joy are so intermittently related
With you, I'm neither forced to keep a smile fixated
Nor am I persuaded to keep family isolated
So I want to indicate it, it may not have been stated
But because of you I render myself happy, naturally elated.

JMS James

JMS James
That's the initial and signature of his very name
Tears he has shed do resemble the rain
Until he learned one day how to deal with the pain.
In the intertwined cloth his story is etched, yet tainted
And I am that colorless canvas awaiting to be painted
To capture his essence, his past and his present
To embrace soft moments and reveal the less pleasant
And he comes to me nightly with thoughts at their loudest
And leaves me by morning with a mind that is soundless
Could it be life's profoundness that pulls at his spirit?
He paints through his soul so that my soul can hear it
And his portrait is print less, his pain leaves him senselessly facing audacity where words are not spoken
And I stand defenseless, as his paintbrush relentlessly strokes the capacity in which he has been broken
The sanguine base builds a collage of rage
A depiction with conviction and emotions engaged
It's not the diction but the friction from pastel to page
I'm his addiction from affliction, I'm there to assuage
Because this life is a stage, or rather, a canvas-like fabric, so thick with his talent of unwavering hues
I want him to value my shadows, glaze my exterior, shape me as a building block and rest on my blues
Because now I see what he views.
He lives incognito, he resembles Filipino in the flickering candle
His hazelnut eyes fall in rhythm with his hands as they feverishly dance and I am his to handle
Because before his paint met my canvas I was branded, as plain
And he was knotted in pain.
Until that night he came to me, drenched in rain
And his tears fell the same and they felt a little strange
And when the rain left existence, only those tears remained
They blended naturally with that sanguine base
And on top lied his blues with every color from his case
Of collections. Although I felt a connection
It was merely a moment, simply just a reflection
From the temporal stress in his chosen direction
Just a spontaneous pick for that night's selection
And I wish I could say that I learned my lesson.
But there is nothing more beautiful than making art with imperfection
Nothing more powerful than a mutual affection
Or letting these colorful strokes act as our protection
Because no one will know the many nights he came
Or how his teardrops in fact resembled the rain
What they'll know is that I'm framed, no longer branded as plain
But with the initial and signature of his very name
JMS James.

Love Lost, Love Gained

How do I describe it?
The best dictionary in the world couldn't define it
Your kindness is timeless, breath-taking like God's storm
I embrace you like water, fully adapting to your form
And I swear, I nearly drowned in plain view
Because I saw the most beautiful man in you.
I prayed for you that night
No words fell out of my mouth, but out of my mind
And were mailed to Jesus by express
I knew that when he received it, he would treat it with the utmost finesse
A mix of dark chocolate and caramel hands clenched tightly
Forming fists against the world while tears streamed lightly
One wrong word uttered could damage you out-rightly
So to support you uprightly I proceeded to politely
Hold you.
Understanding that what I showed you was more important than the words
I told you
You were showered with the welcome of an unwanted guest
Hoping your uncle didn't take his last breath that night.
Hospital doors opened, hopelessly we walked in from the night's drive
Only to find that death walked this path sooner than we had arrived
Dried tears that were once rivers turned into oceans
When we realized God's plan had been set into motion.
I waited. You stepped into the room for a final view of his face.
I watched. Your chest heaved, realizing his spirit left this physical place.
I wrapped. My arms nestled your body, protecting the floor from your pace.
I witnessed. The eternal impact from this moment could never be erased.
Space for you was what I wanted, but you only wanted me near
Broken sobs and a strengthened grip made that very clear
So I will sit with you, hold hands, kiss foreheads and cheeks
Be there during this time because it was divine that you and I should meet
Completely lost without description, my depiction is fragmentary
Beautiful man, help me pull words out of my vocabulary
To describe your heart-shaped innocence
With a perimeter of diligence
Our encounter is no coincidence
So how do I define your significance?
A lifetime. A lifetime.
Yet this is only one season
There are three more to share with you and I have every reason
To place them on repeat in their God-given order
This is a cold winter, but there is silver lining on the border
Or perhaps gold, pure, not plated
If God ever decided that we should be separated
I would be thankful to still have this moment we created
A memory that could never be expired or outdated.
In the stillness of that night, we both locked eyes

Hospital doors closed, trapping the unheard cries
A love lost is a love gained in disguise
Because we should have said goodnight, but we never said goodbye.

Ready or Not

Why don't you tell me about falling in love.
Because I was only told to beware, to behave my emotions
To mature my childishness so as to avoid false notions
Of fairytale conceptions leaving pseudo-impressions
About the lovesick obsession that hides the twist of depression
And, I don't really know if I understand its expression
So many times it does the opposite of growth and progression
But not loving you in itself was a disguisable blessing
That later blossomed into the richness and the realness of my lesson
Don't claim love too soon.
I consider myself a fool for inappropriately using that tool
But really, why don't you tell me about falling in love
Because I wonder if it's real
Or if we lie to ourselves about the truth versus how we really feel
Because I don't buy the phrase "it's indescribable" when I ask about its experience
I neither believe in its ultra-brilliance nor do I trust its magnificence
Some people chase after love, hoping to trim the long distance
But to love is to love with ever fiber and atom of your existence
And I want to know what that feels like
But my walls are too high to let that kind of passion take place
So high that only the logic from my planned romance is able to escape
Give it some time, they say
And I love what time displays.
It showed me how we loved each other under false pretention
Giving our emotions permission to rise from suspension
To change habitual patterns was the focus of our attention
But despising who I became with you was never my intention
But it happened. In the midst of figuring ourselves out
Expecting the same scenery while riding on a different route
You felt more encouraged while I developed more doubt so someone please tell me what all this love is about
I used to turn over to find the comfort of your face
Resting on the green pillows in the warmth of my place
But your imprint on my sheets washes away as it rains
Because it isn't the kind of companionship that God himself ordains for me.
And every time I fill my home, it always ends up vacant
So maybe next time I'll listen when he tells me to be patient
I wanted forever with you, tried to get myself ready
But God pulled me back, see, he just held me steady
And showed me the quick swiftness of the sand
That approaches me as I stand on a desolate land
Lord, get me off this plan of trying to love a man
Without the gift of your brand, without a degree in my hand
I was under self-management, so far from your plan
But I release control from the firm grip of my hand
Because I'm not ready.
Forget what I thought about relational satiety

Hold on to the fantasy, the hype is never the reality
We pick from the same garden while demanding more variety
We are generally an unsatisfied, unscrupulous society
My heart was a phantom of love and I'm past the point of no return
And when I think of me with you, the things that we've been through, the images and memories lay gassed ready to burn
So really what have I learned?
It seems that since we've been together
Loving you forever is what I was afraid of
Love makes no sense
You may feel safe but there is really no defense
So I will wash, lather, rinse without the repeat
Not another trace of love will dare scent me
So feel free to wash me with what love has done for you or what love has put you through at what love has made you do
Why don't you tell me about falling in love?
Because it doesn't seem to fit the thoughts I've already thought of.

Selling the Dream

He greeted me with a hi nice to meet me
And before I could even speak, he tried to determine my needs
He's so good, that smooth talking salesman
Trying to sell me a dream he doesn't even believe in
But like most men do
He tried to close the sale too soon
Spending too much time analyzing my figure
Instead of understanding my emotional triggers
Showing me three carats, assuming I'm a gold digger
Mr. Salesman I happen not to prefer the bigger
Diamonds.
But he confuses me like Simon
And Simon says,
Be with him but understand that he's taken
Don't build a relationship, allow love makin'
Give him attention but don't attach your emotions
Be content in your place with no desire for promotion
To girlfriend, fiancé, or wife
Simon says he wants you in his life
But only on his terms.
So in return, I laugh at his attempts of advancement
Because he only views me as a temporary enhancement
He categorizes me as a quaint accessory
An add-on, an extra, instead of a necessity
Incessantly he courts me around this case full of jewels
Telling me they are beautiful objects of renewal
The price of these diamonds comes with a full set of rules
And I know that those who buy what he sells are the fools
Because he will never wait for them
He'll bate them, date them
And make them feel like purchasing a ring miraculously mates them
This, happily ever after he tries to sell doesn't get to me
Perhaps he should have turned the sale over when he realized he couldn't turn me over in his sheets
But he is the typical and the typical are never satisfied with just a little
But little did he know, he lost me and any loyalty I had on ever coming back
He couldn't meet my needs because of the integrity he lacked
And upon leaving, I carefully derailed from his track
And watched him approach a woman who was wearing all black.
He greeted her with a hi nice to meet her
And before she could even speak, he tried to determine her needs
He's so good, that smooth talking salesman
Hoping that the dream he sells he will one day believe in.

The Other Woman

He handed me his card with a smile of sincerity
Skin smooth to the touch, then his eyes stared at me
Thinking maybe perhaps I was interested in sharing me
As each digit comprising his number gravely dared me
To call him later, see this gentleman had flavor
Mental sapidity, a delicacy to savor
I know some women are sweet so men grab sugar like neighbors
So upon first impression I wasn't swayed by his behavior
And he was certainly no savior, but his presence gave ease
Like the moment after dissonance on black and white keys
Like a world without crime, consequences or fees
Like inhaling the crisp air of a soft Christmas breeze
Understand me,
I breathed him in like nature lives daily
Giving him freedom to candidly sway me
With words, his language would have to obey me
Allowing his actions to court and betray me
But never to display me, I was a well-kept secret
Holding on to fantasies...love? This couldn't be it
So deep within this dream, my reality couldn't see it
And my mind despises him now, no, I refuse to keep it
We sleep through and forsake
The depth love can make
When we pass what is real to appeal to the fake
And my mouth falls to shakes
When it has to form shapes
To articulate the hate I even have for this mistake
Of being the other woman
I should have seen it comin'
Men fall like snowflakes to the ground of a woman
Yet once they reach her, their unique kind of game
Blends in with the others and they all look the same
I blame no gender on how we choose to reside
Hiding our feelings, showcasing our pride
I simply state, it is a dangerous ride
To be seen through his eyes as the woman on the side.

Understand

Will he understand the troubling eyes that follow me around?
Or when I walk into a room, the world mutes from its sound?
Is he capable of comforting the hurt from the blast
Of the everlasting pain from my background's past?
Can he see my frustration when I'm trampled and broken
From screaming to be heard when no word was ever spoken?
He can say he feels my heartache, but my heart aches so much more
He has never seen his ancestors beaten to the floor
Or a bore a child from a rape and be labeled as a horror
Can he tell me he will open unheard of doors
And buy my affection from the walls of a store
When I've struggled with jobs and befriended the poor
Ashamed of my life? I was built to endure
Because he doesn't understand me, why my efforts never fall
I was taught from my history to answer ever call
To break down every wall, to walk the line in every hall
To have the strength to stand tall although I feel this small
And he will never see through the eyes of mine
Which are clustered with anger, which have yet to bear shine
Inside of my mind are twisted and tangled vines
Where I search for a peace I just can't seem to find
Wrapped up in this hatred, I wish to be free
To belong to someone, to love whomever he may be
And just when I think I have altered the perception
I am reminded of my non-white, caramel-like complexion
And our love begins to chip away, each in its own direction
As he smothers my heritage for his own reputation
Too caught up in temptation to handle speculation
This is my humiliation, this everlasting segregation
My reality learns from the slaves, thrives from the past
To love him would position me as an iconoclast
I cannot last on love and the emotions that follow
To abandon my race would cause my own self-sorrow
Now there may be effort in trying to understand
But the only one who can understand a black woman is a black man.

Webster's Dictionary

Black, by definition, yields dirty, soiled, sullen, and wicked
Relating to any various population group having dark pigment
But we have always had to look beyond our limitations
Our complexity expands past this page of explanation
And I quizzically researched the definition of white
Meaning innocent and favorable with pigmentation that's light
Flipping pages to the right, I entertained a dare
Because I looked up beautiful and didn't find black there.
But that definition was never my rendition of beauty
It has everything to do with what we couldn't possibly see
Our skin is dressed in black so no one can see life's stains
The spots may not be visible, but they will always remain
These, scars appear to fade in a time that is significant
Because we are absorbing the abuse and making it look magnificent
Isn't it a masterpiece?
Feel free to marvel at our glow
It is not properly acknowledged and always displayed for show
But beauty doesn't need a second opinion
All it needs is hope and a vision
My beautiful black men and women
Black is beautiful and that is a given.
Black, by my definition, yields impervious and persistent
Relating to a select population group having radiant pigment
Due to Webster's indication, I made my own creation
My black is beautiful, what's your interpretation?

I Am...

Painfully guarded,
Afraid of the feeling a girl might experience while broken-hearted
The sweet dreams involving us have never departed
And while my mind wants to figure out where it all started,
My heart tells me you had me at hello
And there was no need for me to add to your ego
You kept me entertained, told me to let life flow
Your ambition inspired my passion to grow
In return, I wanted you to be my one and only
So you could hold me and show me not be scared of lonely
You set aside my fear, made insecurities disappear
I stared at you and wondered when your halo would appear
With our song on the radio and you on my mind
Memories remind me of how well we are aligned
My emotions smash into you, my guards are sent home
My heart rejoices in knowing that it will never be alone.

*Inspired by I Am...Sasha Fierce Album by Beyoncé Knowles

Give

I'm not afraid of death, but I am afraid of dying while living
Hide the stench of my rotting habits, addictions and misfortunes
Unchained to forgiveness, but handcuffed to silence
Oh, how things could be different.
Fear eats away at me like maggots
Sucks the life out of me like leeches
I desperately want to be free
To do what makes me happy
Stand before you every night
Mic in my hand,
Thought in my mind,
Breath to my rhyme,
Speaking life into your existence,
Giving hope to your situation,
Ultimately letting you know that you are not alone
That, before you go home, you and I will have met minds
Because I know we are all better than the jobs we attend
We hold more weight in life when our passion begins to extend
No, I'm not afraid of death, but I am afraid of dying while living
Sitting eight hours daily in a windowless cubicle,
I wasn't called for this purpose
God doesn't want me to be mirthless
And just like you, my life's not worthless
So I avert this feeling of being shackled like a slave
I am God's child and will always have the freedom that he gave
I speak for change, and I live for difference
What would happen if we ended greed and offered real assistance?
I would sacrifice myself because I'm not afraid of death,
But I am afraid of dying while living
This can all be reversed if we only take subsequent to giving
I'm not afraid of death, but I am afraid of dying without proof that I lived
So in every moment, I have a duty to never withhold, but to give.

Reason

My life is a journey,
Paved by words I've spoken
Flames of envy have tried to burn me,
But I've remained, never broken
See, I have a vision
My ambition never dies,
Among this world I search
For internal tranquility,
Skill and ability,
To rest on love's beautiful surprise...

Cheater

I cheat.
I would say I have cheated,
But it's an incessant thing
Actively I cheat myself out of living my dreams
Yes, I play the game, but no, I'm not ashamed
Because I have company to keep me comfortable
And I don't bother to look into my dreams
Although they are so helplessly searchable
They vie for my attention, but only rarely do I listen
I'd rather focus on the most convenient path that the most satisfying mission
So I cheat.
I would say I'm sorry,
But I know I sneak away on purpose
Trying to avoid the work, doing anything to avert this
Requirement of discipline, setting goals, finishing strong
How unappealing it is to sacrifice for good when I can easily do what's wrong
I am not perfect, but I know I need to change my ways,
Make this habitual cheating a temporary phase,
But it seems to be a cycle, first linked then broken
Which repeats until I change the tone of how I have previously spoken
Remain open to the shift that I can *feel* better than I can *see*
That all the greatness in the world has the right to happen to me
I have cheated in past moments,
But my current can be changed
Remaining loyal to my aspirations,
Never walking back from where I came.

Right

Maybe I've done it wrong
Did we move too fast?
Thinking we could both create a powerful union
From a crumbling foundation,
One that doesn't fully recognize its base,
Love?
Does it act this way?
No, love brings you and me into we,
But we are not individually complete
Not really walking in our purpose,
Not comfortable in our skin
I just start and stop just to begin again
Never having spent adequate time being my own best friend,
Love?
Can it be defined in the end?
It baffles me the way I've used this term
How I claim to feel its presence and yet, still yearn
I wish it moved my soul the way I hear that it can
Instead of me just being your woman and you just being my man
I wish I could provide all you needed
Speak to you in ways unknown
But I know sometimes when we're together,
We have both felt alone
We want to know that we are loved
Understood for how we've grown
We want to call each other King and Queen,
But neither party has taken throne
Maybe I've done it wrong
Moved too fast in your presence
Maybe the excitement blurred my vision
Because I feel blind to your essence
I'm not calling it quits,
But I'm calling it reconstruction
Because our initial approach
Was only under our instruction
I can't deny that I have feelings
Or the fact that we are worth the fight,
But if we're going to pursue each other,
Then it must be done right.

Power

Knowledge is power, but why does power have to act selfishly?
I no longer wish to only operate with the hand that was dealt to me
The rules aren't fair and I'm not blind
I know you play with the trump card every time
You walk with this confidence that you'll always win,
But one who tricks will ultimately be tricked in the end
I won't pretend I'm content with the rules of your game
Because those who lose remain constant, unchanged,
But loss in one area means strength in another
You may rob me of money, but my dreams are uncovered
My spirit has recovered, I see I must have been mistaken
Knowledge isn't power unless the action has been taken
You throw manipulative words right in my direction
You put me down, but I get up and add the hate to my collection
I counteract your hatred with harmony intact
As hate cannot drive out hate, only love can do that
Dr. King fought too hard for my knowledge to be useless
To be used in acts of violence, to be stopped by excuses
Knowledge with action can impede manipulation
And I act because it negates stagnation
I write to release the press of my maker's creation
I speak to reveal that no matter your correlation,
You can plant your dreams in a new location
For stimulation of your mind
For its will is the only real freedom known to mankind
Selfless power produces the ultimate gift
So choose to give abundantly, choose to uplift.

Alive

He retired from the Army
Flag wrapped for his service
On those grounds I thought he'd perish
For his absence made me nervous

Every time I see him
I'm so thankful for our time
Because once I believed
His face would never again meet mine

He fills me with such laughter
Just as he did when we were kids
To make me smile, there was no limit
To the things he did

I treasure all the moments
When we burst into song
Because I know one day forthcoming
This will all be gone

So I keep memories of me playing dolls
And him making all the clothes
I vow to never forget how his rhymes outwit
How they hit, how they ebb, how they flow

I will hold on to the videogames
That occupied our minds
And how, in making cover forts,
The fun we'd always find

Twins by looks, best friends by blood
My brother remains my reason
To never give up, to always look up
To weather every season

And every time I see him
I'm so thankful for our time
He says I woke him up
But he keeps me so vibrantly alive.

Just Friends

Just friends.
Nothing more than casual
No dipping into fantasies, just give me something factual
If you look at it from logic, or in a simple sense of practical
You'll understand, being friends with you is simply unnatural
My actual desire is to love you for a lifetime
To have you trust in my ability as if I were your lifeline
Each mirror I possess reminds me of your face
And your unmatchable laughter, fills this place
But my desire is set on fire when reality hits
Because you have been my friend ever since we were kids
I told you all my secrets and you locked them all away
We never discussed, you never unlocked, even up 'til this day
I know that I can love you better than someone you just met
I'm an expert at taking away the pain and helping you forget
I'm daydreaming of your kiss, but I know things would change
My fantasies stay hidden so that we can still remain...
Just friends.

Mountains and Hills

Laid off from my job
No food in my fridge
My car stopped working
Once I got to the bridge
A note on my door
I can't pay my bills,
But I keep on climbing
These mountains and hills.

I broke up with my boyfriend
Before I knew I was pregnant
The denial of his fatherhood
Grows wildly incessant
This guy didn't love me
He was in it for the thrills,
But I keep on climbing
These mountains and hills.

I have this degree
And I have all of these loans
The idea that was promised
Seems rather unknown
In debt for a lifetime
Just to work on my skills,
But I keep on climbing
These mountains and hills.

Twenty-five years
I've been married to this man
Who wants a divorce,
So I have to change plans
Four kids by my side
Along with God and goodwill
To help me keep climbing
These mountains and hills.

One thing I have realized
On my journey of strife
These mountains and hills
Are in everyone's life
No one's exempt
It doesn't choose sides
Though your hill may come sooner
Than those on their ride.

You may be tired
You may be weak
You may even have a hard time

Feeling your feet,
But never stop moving
No matter what life reveals
We must always keep climbing
These mountains and hills.

Empty

His promises fill me
My soul spills empty
I wait for the pain to imprison me gently
To cuff me, chain me
To strip me, contain me
He clings to my spirit, but only to stain me
I am like a picture he rightfully claims
Reduced in value, seen only in frame
With no one to blame, he's tempted to tame
To shift my position with one of his games
And his tactics are cunning, cryptic, shame-less
He leaves me doubtful, dreary, name-less
To try to contain this, I'm forced to remain this
Ignorant child whose eyes can't sustain this
Thirsty state of human existence
He drinks from the lives of those in resistance
To declare love and leave in an instance
To forever leave me with a burning vengeance
Yet off in the distance, my soul he does swallow
He watches my tears as his eyes I do follow
My body sounds weightless, the inside sounds hollow
I live in this life where my pity does wallow
And although his charming nature can fool honest strangers
I am blatantly aware of his volatile dangers
He is the mood changer, more settings than seasons
I gave him my life without indicative reason
See, I thought it was my obligation to please him
Thinking maybe my touch was enough to ease him
But I was wasting my time, chasing old dreams
Because nothing in this life is as good as it seems
I mean, why did I wait for him to refill me?
After he spilled me so unjustly empty
Yet I waited for him to imprison me gently
Thinking he was the gift that God himself sent me.
Pieces of me crumbled as I stuck to his side
Leaving holes in my life where compassion applied
And there were moments he tried to fill me with pride
But it seeped through the holes from the tears I had cried
From the strength in his tide, from the rules I abided by
Loving him was a form of suicide and I
Can't believe I let a part of me die
Or why I longed to be seen in the gaze of his eye
It's my life he spills and refills and conceals and
Steals the small bit of love that I feel
Too caught up in this pain to instantly heal
His word was my destiny, my unchosen will
But what's real is what lays spilled
I am alive, though my passion is killed

I still desire though my heart has been drilled
And I am still fighting with an improper shield
But this field of dreams I do dream sweetly
Searching for a soul to love me concretely
Secretly I long to love and be loved deeply
But his words will never fill me completely
It's God's love that ensures me, I'll never be empty.

Beautiful Struggle

Last night I had dinner by candlelight, but not by choice so I focused
On the possibility of a more positive and productive prognosis
And others may view this as a poverty stricken diagnosis
My rolled up coins, stove open for heat, and eviction notice
Yeah I know this may sound crazy but I never knew struggle could look so beautiful.
On the brink of pawning my guitar, I'm not afraid of sacrifice
Whether it is victory or vice, it's all a part of life
So I take the strings with ease and strum the melodies
Tuning my pitch to my soul's frequency
To see the wavelengths appear upon the threshold of fear
As it transforms this emotion to nothing but mere
Awe.
And even though I'm uneasy as to how I'm situated
My heart and my mind are completely fixated
On the forthcoming blessings that God has created
With a divinity so pure and a plan so sacred
And I'm done trying to imitate it
His process can't be replicated
But I want him to understand that I am relentlessly dedicated
To the amelioration of issues illustrated
Because it's the thought of getting through it that keeps me motivated
Your arrival is anticipated so continue to test me
And don't let the sins of this world infest me
Or insecurities arrest me, I want you to profess me
To sincerely bless me so I can become the best me
In your eyes.
See I have not time for disguises
Hiding betwixt truths and lies, you are the ultimate high
1 Corinthians 4:4 for I know nothing by myself
My trust is in your hands
My mind now understands
Why you make me struggle.
So I can find you in me again
You were lost in the ideas I had for so many men
While I look five years from now and try to plan ahead of me
You laugh at my attempts, you already know my destiny
You teach me to see differently, I'm not the victim in these situations
I simply surf by life's shore dodging man-made undulations
My purpose is your specialty, pleasing you is my concentration
I am in the safety of your haven because I am purely your creation
So I'm tuning in to your station
Struggles are opportunities for real strengths to surface
And if you don't fight until the end, you chance the lesson being worthless
So I could cry and have pity, but in you Lord I am trustful
I only view this as another day coming out of my struggle.

Beautiful Surprise

It's like yesterday, I didn't even know your name
Now today you're always on my mind
I never could have predicted that I'd feel this way
You are a beautiful surprise.

India Arie sings through my speakers to fill my car with words I crave to retell
With a story that wrapped her in a love spell
I only dream to fall as surprisingly as she fell
As she passed by the charms that commonly sell
To be intoxicated by his voice, his touch, his smell
But I pressed on the pedal to return from the dwell
To the disappointments of knowing myself too well
To the reality of love's unlikely attain
As I drive through the alley slick with yesterday's rain
And arrive within lines of a yellow sun stain
As I shift gears to park, or rather to pain
Because what sustains when the silence remains
Are the thoughts of my soul, too complex to explain
Too intertwined to be plain
But insane to entertain the very core of my being nearly leaves me drained and I'm chained
Set hush to the engine
But the clamor rages and I can't bear to listen
Blindly lost in the tension as my own tears glisten
That song left me deep in an unknown dimension
Shelter from my thoughts is the ultimate goal
I wish they'd console but they only play roles
They only plant holes, I wish I was made whole
But I step into my home with a hold on my soul
So lonely yet lovely, my walk could never tell
The stride of my struggle, no letter could ever tell
The name of my prison where poison has risen
To rid me of reason, all rights and redemption
Through numerous premonitions I saw us stand tall
Or was it that I wanted to see what wasn't there at all
Because inside of this house, behind the tears of these walls
Lies my total destruction, demise, and fall
With minimal rise
I am far from India's beautiful surprise
I'm left envisioning the perfect fit to my soul's size
I'd much rather love and stay than leave bitter goodbyes
But that takes a touch of confidence, will, and compromise
It takes noticing the change of shade as the sun meets my eyes
Instead of giving in to the thirst and quench that hungers at my thighs.
A wise woman once told me, go where you are appreciated, not where you are tolerated
And as the words met my ear

I swear to you, my purpose in this life
Became undoubtedly clear
And every act in this life, whether crass or sincere
Is the exact reason and circumstance of why I'm here
In this quiet room, contemplating my doom or rather my destiny
Because what applies to my life is purpose plus precision
And in my fit to add in passion, I embarrassingly lost my vision
And who should I blame for such ignorant collision
It's the stamp of my name that now plagues each decision
Using division instead of multiplication and addition
My equation proves imbalanced as I solve for my mission
I believe these are trials of a young woman's ambition
To thoroughly transition from an unjust position.
Unlike India, I have yet to receive what my prayers have requested
That one to heal my soul, I feel divinely tested
Clouds of hope have come, I've punctured, pulled, and pressed it
But this is the base of emptiness in which my rage has nested
Hope still survives around the perimeter of love's denial
Because I wonder if there is one that gives reason to my smile
Love hasn't forgotten, it's just simply not my time
To fine dine or sip the finest red wine
For now I'll listen to the smoothest, sweetest, slickest line
But when I see that sign, I'll go after what's mine.
The night has left quickly behind an emerging rise
The sun brings back the color which the moon took from my eyes
I dress in modest confidence, trying freedom on for size
And leave my lonesome house in search of a beautiful surprise.

Dream or Reality?

What's the difference between a dream and reality?

Badly, I want to know,

A dream is a series of thoughts, images emotions occurring when we are asleep,

But this can happen when we are awake,

Wait, what is the difference between a dream and reality?

Reality the quality or state of being real,

But, I feel my dreams, I understand

When my eyes are closed and my heart beats slow

Like a new born baby enjoying a warm bottle,

Calm, cool and relaxed,

I dream of that dance with that guy, I cry when he leaves, I can feel his hand slipping away,

I swear it's just like reality

(you see)

I question this moment,

Are we awake or are we sleep?

Slip on a pair of jeans right now,

Because this is reality,

But I promise I can do the same in a dream,

So tell me what is the difference between a dream and reality?

This all can seem real but it could be false,

'Cause we could all be in a room sleep with our hands crossed,

Why couldn't this be a figment of our imagination?

Why can't we all be a sleep waiting to awaken,

Maybe you're thinking to yourself,

I wouldn't envision my life being this way,

I wouldn't want to struggle or my grand ma to pass away,

Would if I said it was a cover up,

And everything can't be perfect because if it was we would see the big

Picture, which is bigger than us,

We fuss and cuss, get extremely sad when our love ones pass away,

But it could be that they woke up and entered into real reality,

Sadly we are stuck in a dream,

<u>Now that's the difference between our dreams and reality.</u>

Danced to the Beat

The beat of the drum,
Has broken,
The ocean,
Is still,
I feel nothing,
When there was something,
How did the rhythm stop?
I must have forgot,
Myself in you,
Whose words were as smooth,
As a drum's top,
I did not stop,
Listening to your rhythm,
I danced to your beat,
My soul felt it,
With joy,
You toyed,
With me,
Like the tango with a kiss
Now I can see,
Like a hawk,
That I gave you permission,
By saying yes,
To this dance,
You spun me so slow,
Didn't realize
I was in motion,
You dropped me,
But caught me,
To drop me,
Again,
Spin, drop, twist, twirl,
I was caught up in your world,
Tangled,
But I ain't mad at ya,
I recognize my beat,
And it plays,
In a Different place,
On a different drum,
In a different world,
Spin that!
You can't,
'Cause I'm the composer,
Of the beat, intertwined with the song for so long
I danced with you,
Why?
When I,
Can dance,

My best alone,
To my own,
Song,
Rhythm, beat
See,
I have embraced it,
And you noticed,
But can't join,
The dance,
Understand,
So you stand,
There,
Tapping your feet,
Listening to my beat,
Only wanting to dance,
With me,
But you've missed the beat.

Started To

Fear = Danger

Danger was his name,
Never explored his dreams,
Never proclaimed,

Never took that step,
Never knocked on that door,

Never,
He never,
Wanted more,

Always thought he couldn't,
Always thought who cares,

Always feared he'd fail,
And he was almost there,

Always thought the worst,
When he was the best,

Always thought he could,
But never took the test,

Always rested,
But never got up,

Started to feel the rage,
Of not being enough,

Started to think,
But never finished the thought,

Started to feel his nothing,
Was all his fault,

Started to see her dreams,
All pan out,

Started to feel regret,
Without a doubt,

Started to pout and scream,
Started to feel closed in,

Started to feel like a loser,
When he was born to win,

Started to feel she was leaving,
When she is right there,

Started to look at her,
With thoughts,
Of life's not fair,

Started to lose all hope,
Like he was falling behind,

He started, but never finished
That never crossed his mind.

Feeling a Death

The day seemed odd,
My mind thought strange,
My heart stopped,
(Pause)
Every time I thought of your name,
The air thinned out,
The walls closed in,
My ears couldn't hear,
Far nor near,
The day was bright,
But,
My soul was blue,
All I could think,
Was,
Not you,
My eyes felt heavy,
My vision blurred,
The amount of tears,
Couldn't express,
My hurt,
Your body's untouchable,
Your thoughts unheard,
Your smile,
Only,
In my mind,
Now,
Your distance so far,
In memory so close,
Too many things,
That I'll miss about you most,
Time's going on,
And so are you,
As long as I'm living,
Your memory lives too,
My dreams
So vivid,
Of you at night,
It's hard to accept,
That you left,
Our side.

Expressed Drive

My body lacks movement,
It's a stiff as a log,
And my mind,
Jogs steady, but slow,
I can't control,
What I dream,
But,
I can't express it,
Manifest it,
So I pressed this,
Man-made ,
Object,
On this,
Bright white pad,
And be glad,
I can,
Move to prove,
I can,
I will,
And I am
When I dream,
I see it,
So,
I feed it,
And,
It will grow,
Over time
Because,
I
Have God,
To guide,
Me,
Through the storm,
Only God knows,
What I've endured,
I will not ignore,
The gifts,
He's given me,
You see,
I sleep,
To dream,
And awake,
To accomplish,
You can't stop this,
Because I got it,
And it comes from the Lord,
So I ignore,
The negative remarks,

To start,
My positive journey,
Learning,
And earning,
What some can't see,
He feeds me drive,
And
Clothes me in courage,
He whispers in my ears,
Not to fear,
What he has for me,
So I stand on my feet,
And lift my hands high,
Ready to fall down,
To get up,
And touch the sky.

Face of a Dove

I have to put on my face.
Get ready for the world,
I have to put on my face.
Who cares if it's fake?
It's just important
That I put on my face.
Where's my make up
That makes up my face?
My mascara that stops my tears from falling,
The foundation that lays down the foundation of my day,
Because,
Underneath it is three shades of gray.

I place
On eye shadow,
Because,
It hides,
My life battles.
I'm sad though,
But,
Society says put on a smile.
Because no one wants to see someone that's down,
So I,
Put on a smile that was upside down,
And simply turn it right side up,
But wait,
I can't start my day without lining my eyes
That you say shine,
But are not really mine.
Because mine have to hide,
To show that my spirit's high,
Blush covers up my natural rosy cheeks,
Because the fake roses are always brighter,
Verses mine that are sometimes weak,
You can't see me,
Because,
I have on my face.

My face was fake,
But it's becoming,
More permanent
Everyday.
I just place on my lipstick,
Because it works with my smile,
And my real one's not as gorgeous as a Barbie doll's,
But enough about me now,
I'll just carry on my day with my one million dollar smile.

Wow,
Today, once again,
I have to put on my face
That's immaculate to the world,
I have to,
But don't really want to,
Become a cover girl.
Covering this girl.
That is hardly seen,
That screams.
Who's the real me underneath?
Don't you see?

I have to put on my face.
You know.
The one
My mother and father made
That society simply replaced.

Change

Change,
It's here,
Starting with the way,
The days are aligned,
The world is designed,
To change.

The people,
Think the same,
Feel the same,
The pain,
Others feel,
From the repetitive beat,
Repeat,
Repeat,
History,
Where is the change?

Me, Lord,
For I am willing,
Make me new,
What to do,
In the world,
Of the unforgiving,

Cleanse me, Jesus,
The virus,
Is here,
I do not fear,
But I need not,
For what the world has got,

STOP!
The negative thoughts,
In others, Lord,
I pray,
They come to you,

The Miracles,
The healing,
Forgiving,
You do,

It's more than proof,
That you are near,
Hear me clear,
World,
Our Father,

Will come,
In the flesh,
And,
The rest,
Will be history.

You're Frozen

You're Frozen,
More Frozen than ice,
You cannot see,
The severity,
Of the situation,

Too busy frozen
On the sideline
Hatin'.

Hatin'
My goals,
Downgrading my dream,

So busy trying,
To get me to fold,
Losing sight of your dreams,
I breathe,
Slow,
As you try
And try,
To break me down,
But every push,
I get strong
Levitating from the ground,
You pound,
At my heart,
Trying to stop the beat,
But,
It will sound loud
Even when I'm 6 feet,
You see,
Every move you make,
That involved bringing me down,
The Lord looks at you,
And puts on my crown,
Don't frown at me
'Cause I'm smiling at you,
Because no matter what you do,
I will get up,
And you'll still
Be,
Frozen,

More frozen than ice
Standing
On the sideline
Hatin'.

Hatin' my goals
Downgrading my dream,
You lost
Everything
By making
Your job title:

Hatin' on me.

Outside the Window

Scream,
Hit,
Cry,
Why?

Do your lips,
Spit,
Out,
Jagged swords,

I,
Ignored,
It,
The first time,

I let,
Swords fly,
Over my head,

You said,
You'd feed me,
Positively,

But,
I've gotten,
Rage,
And,
Pain,
That you've claimed,
Ages ago,

I'm not the darkness,
On top of your shadow,

But you continue,
To battle me,

Bringing swords,
To a meet and greet,
About peace,

I see the pain
In your fight,
But don't
Fight
Me.

Fight

The negative energy,
You're giving me,
And yourself,

Don't fight
Alone,
Seek help,

Scream,
Cry,
Shout,

Lord,
Help me,
Please,

Scream,
Pray,
Cry,
Speak,
On your knees,

And
You will
See a change,

Your view,
Step outside,

Don't let
The walls,
Close in.

While inside,
Step down from pride,
Everyone needs a hand,

You will never fly
When chained,
To pain,
Gain,
Control,
Of yourself,

You can't
Help others,
Until you
Help self.

The Man With The Plan

The seeker found a thought,
The thought found the dream,
The dream found the man,
That plans,
Everything,

He acts on the thought,
It wasn't hard to do,
His mind saw a VISION
He'll soon execute.

His vision made sense,
When seen in his mind,
But failed
Over one-hundred times.

The man tries again
Despites how he feels,
Because
No matter
How many failed attempts,
He knew his dream was real.

He feels
It in his soul,
He has control,
Of his mind,
He wouldn't let
His
Let-downs
Push his dreams aside.

He tried
Every day,
Morning
And night,
He'd worked too hard
To,
Give up the fight.

It happened
It's here,
His great vison
Shines,
It all happened
For him
After two-hundred tries.

A Hold

I am trading
Sleep for you,

I'm in so deep.
My thoughts
Think
Of you,

Refuse to stay away
You want me,
Every day,
You demand,
My attention,
And
I listen.

To every demand
Programmed
To take your orders,
Maybe
For the rest of my life,

Something inside,
Draws me to you

What should I do
Or should I do,
Anything at all?
You haven't let me fall,

You help me clear my mind,
When I think a thought
And express,
That's my rest,

Why dream
When I can deliver
My dreams to you.

Why dream
When I can express
My dreams to you,

Are the good and bad,
The beautiful and ugly,
And you want me,
And I want you,

Pen,
Paper,
Thought,
Poetry,
Pen,
Paper,
Thought,
Poetry
Is holding me,

Too tight
Day and night,
Night and day,
I have something
To express and say,

I pray to God,
Then,
I come to you,
Pen,
Paper,
Thoughts,
Poetry.
Has got,
A hold of me.

Mind Heated

Mind heated
Heart pounding,
Not stopping,
To think,

I think,

I misplaced,
Common sense,
With,

Pain and adrenaline

I feel this emptiness,
Inside,
When I decided,
To,

Let a person control
My feelings,
I'm not dealing,
With God,
But the Devil inside,

When
I,

Run up
To slap you
In the face,

Frustration,
Enters my soul
Because I can't control,
How you were raised,

Or
What you say,

So I become you,
Wild and Untamed,
To relate

My hands get heavy
As it changes its form

My fist,
Is how I'm handling,

Disrespect,

How can I rest?

Knowing I hurt you,

But you,
Hurt me,
Is what I think,

So I let that thought carry on,
Inside.

So I can replace,
Wrong with right,

But I'm wrong,

By becoming you,

I should have reacted,
In a different way,

I should have chosen
The Godly way,

I should have said,
I love you,

My sister,
My brother,
And walked away.

Speak the Truth

Speak the truth,
And,
Your soul,
Will not fold,

Trying to control,
A lie

Why
Let the serpent hold your tongue,
The war has begun
Corrupt communication
Proceeds to be your
Outlet,

You sat down
And thought of twisted words,
It hurts
Inside
To see you
Cry
Out
For attention

There's something
You're missing,
Love from above,
Could heal this pain
Refrain from negativity
Open your mind
To the Creator

And
He will favor
You

Blessings
Will
Pour
Over
Your life
Like
Honey

How lovely life,
Would be
If we didn't
Corrupt communication.

She Rose

She rose,
Early in the morning
To go to work,
She rose,
To go
To school,
Back hurting,
Eyes heavy,
Still,
Ready,
To rise,
Dream on hold,
Heart of gold,
Nowhere to go,
But,
Shows,
Courage
She will flourish,
While carrying,
A load of dreams in her head,
And
Children in her arms,
Heart on guard,
To raise,
What she's claimed,
And named
At birth,
Her children
Are worth,
More than,
She could imagine,
So she,
Had to make it happen,
Her dreams,
Must come true,
In order,
To water
Her seeds
She has to be
Their food,
Her life
Starts passing her by,
So she drives,
Through the pain,
And
Heartache,
Passing through
Each stop sign,

Full speed,
Ready
To fulfill,
Her needs to care,
For her seeds.

My Blackbird

My blackbird
Will fly,
Her wings will open wide,
And,
I will embrace the strength,
Of my Blackbird,
I will not cage her,
For the world shall witness her beauty,
Duty lies in her soul,
So she will grow,
With the wingspan
That no one has ever seen,
You should hear her sing,
My Blackbird,
Is unique,
With no limits
And her expectations are high
She will be the wisdom to the nation,
My Blackbird,
Will not only fly,
Her wings will reach new heights beyond the sky,
You will fly,
And I will be,
By your side,
Blackbird,
Her heart will care for others,
And she will hover
Over the innocent,
With the protection of the Lord,
You will be floored,
And will not ignore,
My blackbird.

I Never Felt the Need to

I never felt the need to
Confide in you,
I always felt the need to
Speak the truth,

Proof,
Of the Lord
I didn't look for,

I fast forward and rewind
In my mind,
And decide,
That He has been and will be
And we will see
Soon enough,

I cuffed anger
And put it in the back seat,
Along with bitter,
But I kept sweet,

I believe in the Almighty
More than
I believe you,
And that a piece of me being true,
You should too,

But you will do
As you please
Because
We see,
Different

And that's OK,

I will say,

I will forever
Remain
A believer

And I will
Confide
In the way of the Lord,

I agree with every command,
And his book I understand,

But I don't get you
And that's a piece of me being true,
You should too,

Once again,
I never felt the need to confide in you,
Because I always
Looked to the
Lord for truth.

9 to 5

I worked for you day and night,
And you paid me,
With a check,

Not getting rest,
I pressed
The time clock
As I watched
My dreams
Be put on hold,
To get the gold
Dollar,

I was bothered,
Pushed to my limit,

But I stayed with it,

To pay my way,

I stayed away
From my daughter,
So hunger,
Wouldn't exist,

I missed her learning,
Working
For the gold,

Am I the blame?

I'm making an exchange

Time for money,
I could be working,
On a dream,

But I feed,
Your family
With labor,
That you control,

Pushing my goals
Underneath
The sea,
So deep
I can hardly
See them,

As they grasp
For life,

How could I
Linger,
In your corporation,

When I should be making
My own?

You own me,

My time,
My mind,
And voice,

I can't avoid,
The void,
I feel

Working my 9 to 5
So I quit.

You Decide

You despise,
Wisdom,
And deny,
Instruction,

Despite your circumstances,

I'm not understanding,

Why?

Do you have the ultimate plan,
To not only stand,
But,
Levitate?

Let's make the choice to absorb
Positive advice,

Put your pride aside,
And open your mind,

I Care
Because you express concern,

I learn,

That you only speak
Of things,

Yet
Not doing

Proving
Nothing to yourself,

You dealt
Out your wants,

But not
Taking the time,

To put the work,
To use,

You abuse

Your dreams

By saying that you will pursue,
But never do,

You bring a lie to life
Every day,

Why treat your dreams that way?
Pay
Close attention
To what you're missing,

Everything you *want* to do,
You
Lose
A piece
Every day
Because
You decide

In your mind
That
Your dreams
Won't be achieved.

When the Time Comes

When the time comes,
Our souls will meet.
The lights,
Will dim,
And,
I will swim,
In the goodness,
Of the Lord with you,
Our hearts will bind,
And you will find,
Me,
I will feel your soul
Tugging
At mine,
Inside and out
There,
Wouldn't
Be doubt
That we belong,
God will place me,
In your arms,
And we
Will ring the alarm,
To alert the world,
That we are here,
And God is near,
But do not fear
For the time has
Come to
Make a change
And
Obey
His demands,
We will get the
World to understand,
That you and I,
Can
Build a house
That can't
Be
Broken or moved,
And that
They can, too,
We can choose
Not to,
Get lost in sin
We can win!
From within,

And have
Internal joy,
Without feeling
A void
We will not toy,
With one's emotions,
But
Move like the ocean
At once,
Together
You
And I
Will become one soul
With God in control.

What Could I Say?

What could I say?
This is your life,
I cry because you decide to...

Misuse your resources
Of course
I'm upset,

The rest
Could care less
About you,

I'm telling you,
What to do
Because,
I love you,

You prove, haters right,
When you decide,
To do nothing,

I'm wanting
Your gifts to shine,
But you hide them
Swimming in a pool
Of pain,
I just want you to
Claim
Your destiny,
I see you crawling,
Wanting to stand,
But stumbling down,

I want you to stand
Proud,
With your
Crown on your
Head,
I want you to,
Understand,
That you can,
Break though
The hurt,
And know your worth
More than you dream,
Jesus paid
The price for you,
You're everything.

Lord Save the King

Lord save the king,
For the people have turned,

They have learned,
False information

Now,
They're waiting
For my fall,

I saw it coming,
But not
So soon,

What shall I do,
Lord,
I look to you.

Eyes
Look at me
Full
Of misunderstood hate,

They continue to paint
Self-hate,
As their portrait,

Lord let them,
Paint beauty

For You have designed
Them in the image of You,
Almighty,
Have them accept You,

I pray to You that my mind and heart not judge,
Because I will be

And Lord I ask
Ahead of time
To please have mercy,
On me,

I've seen
Acts of hate,
I've heard
What I did not expect,

I rest
With my chest to the sky
Never in wonder
What my enemy will do,

But with You
In my
Mind,
Body,
And spirit,

I witnessed,
The toughs
Speaking
Of my downfall,
Wanting
To see me crawl
With my head low,

But I will
Not follow their slithers

I will follow Your command
And demands
Because You are my King.

Sitting at the Park

Sitting at the park,
As the sun shines upon my face,
I face the wind,
It hits me and jogs my mind,
The side of you I knew,
Had vanished
Without a trace,
Someone erased to replace
You,
I never knew who,
It is a mystery that I may never solve
Who was involved?
What were their names?
I refrained,
From research,
It hurts,
To accept,
The steps
That you have taken
It's made you cold,
Where did you go?
I see your shell,
But can't tell that you're inside,
I'm trying to find you,
But
The fog
Covers the wall,
That you're behind,
I found my reflection,
While looking for you,
I knew you were gone
But I
Vanished too.

I'm Not Attracted To You Anymore

I'm not attracted to you anymore,
I hope you feel bad,
That,
I've made that,
Clear
And you fear that,
You will never,
Ever,
Fall in love,
Again,
I hope I win,
At,
Making you feel,
Low
So low,
That you can't,
Go
To another,
I hover,
Over you,
To continue to,
Remind you,
That,
I'm not attracted to you anymore,
Please endure that,
I want you to have,
That,
Embedded,
In your mind,
Because,
I'm,
Upset,
That,
You walked away,
One day,
And
I can't take,
It again,
I want to win,
In,
Every way,
Mistreat you,
To have you,
And you,
Want to walk away,
So I say
I'm not attracted to you anymore,
Don't ignore me

Let my words feed your soul,
Because,
I am low
And I want you to feel the same,
You claimed,
I was the one,
But you punched
Me in the heart
Although
We fall apart,
I desire
And
Admire you,
But I hide the truth,
Within
In my soul,
And mumble a lie,
I'm not attracted to you anymore
But
That's,
A lie.

The Force

My eyes are heavy,
My mind thinks sleep,
My knees are weak
Can barely speak,

Don't want to think
My mind is blank

Just want to
Say

Good night,
But I fight,
The force,

Ignoring
My limits,
I fill
My temple
With black caffeine,

To push back
My rest,

I slept,
Zero hours,
And
Every part of me says
Shut down

For just
5 minutes,

But I'm not quitting

Addicted
To awake

I pay,
The price

I fight my body,
To procure my hobby,
In the lobby

I stay up
Pumped
To

Accomplish a goal,
Which has gained control
Of my Health,

No sleep
Forget to eat.

I only see the light
At the end of the tunnel
No pain
No sleep
No time to be weak or
Sleep when I can see,
The light,

So I fight
The force,
Simply
Because
I want more.

I Don't Want to Hear

I don't want to hear
Another lie,
So why decide to listen,

It's not my mission,
To put up
With the mess
I have the rest,

Of my life,
To decide
Where my time,
Goes,

And it won't
Be to your negative thoughts,

I'll walk away
Before you say
A word and turn me away,
From Christ.

I will scream
I love you

Before
You
Place hate on
The tip of your tongue,

I will sit on your rage
With a hand full of hearts,

Killing you with kindness,

And will not deny
That
I did the crime,

Why?
Be angry
When the outcome
Is danger,

Let's be strangers
To lies
And best friends
With the truth,

Let's lose,
Jealous,
And replace it
With
Confidence,

I'm stopping this
Right
Now

I won't put
You down,
I won't fight your way,

I won't say
Harsh words
To make you feel weak,

I won't hit you
To see you fall
To your knees

I will be,

The band aid to your wound,

I will pray for you
To have a brighter day
Minus the rain,

I will frame your
Self-image
And hang it on my wall,
Because I think
You all are beautiful,

I will not lose
You to bitterness, sadness or rage
I will walk away
Dragging you behind
With love chains

And we will both walk away
From negativity,

To see
The son of God,
Who will shine
Upon our lives.

Let the Wickedness

Let the wickedness,
Of the wicked,
Come to an end,

Let songs
Display truth
And proof
From within

Let the women
Find love
From their Father
In the sky

Let the leaders lead
With God
In their heart, spirit, and mind,

Let us find
Joy in the storm
Let's rejoice in pain
Because God is testing us,
Now
And when we pass we will gain,
Let's claim
Happiness before it exists
Let's live by faith,
Not
Only
By vision
Let's do the unexpected
Let's respond with love
Let's act as our Father would,
So we can thrive above,
Let us hug our enemies
Because
It's what
They need
Let's sing of positive,
Not
Negative things

Let's lead
The nation
With our gifts
Let's use them
With God's intent

Let the wickedness
Of the wicked
Come to an end

Let's treat our brothers and sisters all the same
Because we all live, love, and bleed the same,
Let us claim victory
Because
We know it is near,
Let's not fear
To save God's people
Let's listen to all the good God tells us
To defeat the evil

Let's read to know the difference between
Right and wrong,

Read to see the wolf
To know
Where you belong
Don't move with the world,
But move with God,
Then you will see,
He will open,
Your eyes.

We Journeyed into the Wilderness

We journeyed into the wilderness,
Forgetting the Lord,
We turned our backs,
Did not look back,
At,
The Lord,

We ignored advice,
Did not stand by
His side
We denied,
The Lord,

We danced in sin,
Having kids,
Without
The Lord,

We poured our love on one another,
But did not cover,
The Lord,

We ignored his direction,
Which
Kept us guessing,
Where is
The Lord?

We swore
With swords
In our hands
Because
We did not stand
With
The Lord,

We spoke in rage,
Accepted pain
Because we did not
Claim
The Lord,

We flew so fast
We ran right past
And did not grasp,
The Lord,

We became afraid
Of the life we made,
Without
The Lord,

Then
Jesus poured
His blood on us
To keep us near
The Lord,

We poured our hearts,
Which were apart,
Until we seen
The Lord,

We grew so fast
And
We asked
Please,
Forgive us
Lord,

We ran right past
The world
Of pain
To run and
Gain
The Lord,

We say
Goodnight,
But
Do not fight
Because
We trust
The Lord.

You Asked Me

You asked me,
Where's my God,
In the midst,
Of the storm,

I say

My,
Rock,
Is next,
To,
Me,

He,
Sinks,

Into my bones,
And,
Grabs a hold,
Of my soul,

He is,
Still,
In control

He is bold,
And,
Knows,
My limits,

Who is
This enemy
When,
Compared
To my God?

Non-existent,

I'm existing,
In spirit and flesh
Because
His flesh perished,
For me,

So you ask me
Where is my God,
In the midst of the storm,

I state,
My,
Rock,
Is next,
To,
Me,

Always has been
Always will be.

With My Soul

With my soul,
I have,
Desired you,

Within,
My,
Spirit,

I can see,
That we,
Are to be,

In peace

I stand,
Next to
My mate,

I claim,
Love,
And it,
Embraces me,

I can see,
Our story,
Before
It begins,

I spin,

In laughter
Beside you,

I guide you,
But
You guide me,

In the deepest
Way,

I can say,
I love you,
And feel it,
Too,

I can be
Without,
But

Still
Feel,
Near
To
You

No proving,
That we match,
God,
Attached
Us both,

Before
I saw you
I had
Already known

Your name
I did not hear,

But
In your eyes,
I'd find
Your soul,

When I saw
You,
I felt
A pull
In myself,

I can tell
I'm
A part
Of you,

You are
A part of me,
That's the way,
Our Father
Intended
It to be,

You, God
And me,
We

Will....

I Don't Want Another Dream

I don't want another dream,
That sits
Under a rock,

I want to expose it,
And show what I got

I want stop,
Until
It is all
Revealed,

I want to heal
The dreams
That have been
Broken
And
Ignored

I want to open the door,
But
Step Inside

I want to
Open my eyes
And mind,

I
Have to perfect
My skill
So that when it's ready

I can open it,
Like a gift
That
Pops out confetti

I'll move steady,
But swift

So I can lift
Up
Perfection,

Resting
Is for the dead
And
I

Am
Alive

I was designed
To deliver
God's message

And after
My calling
Is
Complete

He'll be calling me,

So I
Constantly speak
Life
Into my skill

That is
Almost,
But not quite
Ready,
But
I will soon
Reveal,

The gifts,
That displays
The message,
And truth,

I'll open my gift
To lift up
My Lord.

I will open my gift
To lift up
Me and you.

I will open them
That is the truth.

Your Loyalty Does Not Lie With Me

Your loyalty does not lie with me.
Which is fine,

But don't
Start to care
When I leave you behind,

You denied me once
And that's all it takes

I can't wait,
Or take my
Time with you

Because
My time
Is what I can't lose

I proved
That I cared,
Tried to give you love,
But you
Drug, slapped, and kicked my opinion,
Murdered my feelings
Now you're missing

Me,

But
I forgot
Your
Shoulder shrugged,
Mixed feelings and shade,
I forgot,
Like you,
And
Turned away,

I prayed
You'd understand
Your betrayal

So
Now you do,

Because
Suddenly
You want me

To be loyal to
You.

I did all I could
I was on your team,
But
You
Chose to be selfish
And display
Greed

You kicked me at my lowest,
Didn't extend
A hand

Still 'til this day
I don't
Understand,

Now you're trying to get me
To get you,

Funny how the tables
Turned
On you,

My month has
Opened wide

'Cause even
I'm in shock,

I stopped traffic
When I heard the news,
Sasha Dixon
New and improved.

I'm in a Constant Battle

I'm in a constant battle
With my heart and mind,

One tells me to take a chance,
The other says
Leave it behind.

My heart is my weakest
And I'm trying
To be strong.

So where does
My heart
Really belong?

It tells me to stop
And care for you,

But
What would that really do?

My mind knows the answer
And so do I,

It will
Slow me down
And bring tears
To your eyes,

So I
Must
Shut the door
On love
And call it
Quits

Because
I've done it.
And
Quiet with it,

I can set
And control my mind,
But
My heart
Has
A special design,

It can't be controlled
And there's
No logic to it

With love
What's the point
To it?
There's ups and downs
And
Different views
Sharing space,
Sounds like
I'll lose,

I wake up happy,
But
Love could
Alter that,
My mind
Is stating
Truth with facts,

It is winning the war
Because
The facts
Are hard to ignore,

My heart is fading
It may soon disappear,

I can't say
I'm sad,
But
It may feel weird.

Tittle Trail Mix

There are too many things
Going on,

Everything's all mixed up,

Can't hardly see
Which one
Belongs with me,

I look and see
A face like mine,
But
I realize
We are different

I'm
So confused
And lost in the mix
It's getting hard
To deal with,

There are people,
But none match
Me,
I'm beginning to think
I'm in the wrong space,

I can't wait to get out.
How did I
Get mixed up
In this crowd?

And how will
My match find me
If we are not in the same field.

I feel
Out of place
Just wanting
To be in the
Same place
With you

What can I do?
I can't escape,

It seems like the same
People are surrounding me,

I can't see any other
Because they
Cover me

Won't let me be
Myself,

I belt
Out your name,
But you do not claim
Me

I think
You're gone,
I think you escaped

I think someone erased
You
Or you're just
Sitting in the mix,
Trying to fit in.

I can lend
You a hand

And we can
Escape
The mix.

They Did Me Wrong

They did me wrong,
But
You've done me right,

Stayed by my side
Despite
My sins,

I win
Inside and outside
Because of You,

I can do
Anything
I set my mind to

Because You
Are in my soul.
All wrapped up,
Twisted,
And tangled
Inside

Outside
My soul

I Failed
To find You.
I look
In their
Eyes
And
It's Your
Absence
I'd find,

Why
Won't they
Except
You
Are good
In all things,

I'll stay true
To Your mission
And plan,

Some may not

Understand,

I'll stand
And wait
Years
For you,
Whatever
You want me
To do.

To carry out Your
Plan,

I weep
When I think
Of Your glory,
I could praise you all night,

Because when I
Raise Your name
In praise

I gain
Self-worth,
Confidence, and glory,

I worry
Less
Because
I rest
Next to You,

Each morning
You give me wings
To fly
And complete Your
Plan
My dream
Is for others to
Understand.

Keep Smiling

Keep smiling although
Your Father is gone,

Keep looking to the sky
Cry

If you must,

Trust,
The Lord
And He will not ignore
You,

Prove
Victory,
Don't claim defeat,

Speak
Power
And it
Will be.

Keep smiling although
Your mother is gone,

Because she is not in pain,
Pick up and look high
Because she wouldn't want it
Any other way

Say glory Lord
You are
And I will repent

And He will see
You

And you will
See them,

Stay hopeful,
Believe in faith,

If you do

It's you
The Lord
Will claim,

Fame,
Power, and money
Won't open
His heart,
But neither
Will sorrow and pain,

Refrain
From the world,
For it is full of
Wicked,
Take God's word and drown
In it,

Stay true
To your mission
And you will go far,
It's hard
To
Keep smiling although
Your daughter is gone,
Please,
Stay strong

You long
For her
And God longs for you ...

So you
Can
Keep smiling
Because your Father
Never left.

I Shared

I shared,
Childish laughter
And
Tears with you,

Now they're left alone,

I sang
A song
Of joy
With small amounts of pain,

I gained
Happiness
When surrounded
In your presence
I wasn't,
But felt so close
To heaven

I spent 7 days
With you
Before you vanished
From earth

In those 7 days
My soul
Was beyond hurt,

I shared truth
With you,

You always spoke your mind,
Never had to hide
What was inside,

I shared a bond with,
You
Somehow
We were connected
I felt it,

But
Never
Expressed it,

I went months
Without you

Always wanted you near
That was one of
The things
That
I feared,

You were honest
With me,

Did not hold
Your feelings hostage,

You
Stopped
And shared your love
With me,
But
I did not let it be,

I was free
With you,
I had no control,

I could dance
With no
Rhythm
Sing with
No notes

I would float

On cloud 9
With you,
And
I still held back

You asked for my head
But I danced
By your side

Because
My mind
Stopped
My heart
From my
Feelings inside,

You died
On the seventh day,

And I could not
Share my pain,

I sang to God
For you,

To fight depression,
I prayed
To gain
My lesson,

I'm pressing on
For you
To share
What we once had.

I grabbed my
Soul.
From the enemy
I did not
Give you
Up,

I lifted up

For you
My dear friend
You were
And will be
When God carries
Me home

I have grown
For you
And we will
Shine
When God decides,
It's our time.

Just Be Glad

Just be glad
The sun rose
Like the rose
In the garden

It's a beautiful sight
I saw the light this morning
I'm glad for that,

I sit up
With sleep
In my eyes
And glide
Across my room,

To choose
What to wear,
I stare
In the mirror
Before I wash my face

And believe
That I am blessed
To see
To breathe
To walk and talk,
For you,
I'm able to do

So much

And I'm glad for that
I sat
On my porch
To
Take a look at the world,
I curled up
And felt so small,

Then
I thought again
And felt big,

I pinned
Myself to the couch
To watch TV,
Only to see
Lies

Channels 1, 2, and 3
Owned me
For 15 minutes

Before
I called it quits

I went
To work
Instead of watching my
Seed
Because
Money is a necessity

I work for a man that I hardly know,

And that's the way the world goes,
Hate in the work place
Peace at home
Everyday
I'm on a routine
It doesn't seem
Right

So I fight
The norm
And explore
My opinions

Stopping
At doors
Of success
So I can
Finally rest
In peace
And
I'll
Be
Glad for that.

Our Lips and Ears

Our lips and ears
Have the power

The power to take in
And release,

If your lips slip out
The wrong information,
You could be facing
Pain,

You could claim
Life
Or death
By what you speak

If you see
Knowledge
And come across
The wrong information,
You could be facing
Danger,

Will you be safer
Keeping
Your thoughts
Locked in your mind?
Or will
You forever hide
The truth

Trying to lead the people
By what you know
Could go against
A plan

That only you may understand
Based
On
What you witnessed

You could have to make
A life or death decision,

Winning the battle
But losing the war,

You have to fight

You can't ignore

Luke warm
Is not an option

Either
You're being stopped
Or
Stoppin'

But
You got
The power
And
It's up to you
What you
Will
Or won't do,

To be a hero
Is to be alive
To be quiet
That's when
You've died.

If You Love Him

If you love him,
Tell him now!
For he is your
Friend
So let him
Understand your love.

Hugs can show it
And

So can a smile
Let's hug
Our friends now!

Embrace his glow,
Add to his shine

I'll love my friend,
Before
He dies

I'll sing this song
To a body that breathes,

I'll bow to the Lord
On my knees
To please
Protect my friends,

I'll stand
In the cold
To cheer
You on,

I won't
Let down
My friend
I'll carry on

I'll lift up loyal
If it weighs
Me down

And surround
My friends
With smiles,

I'll motivate the

Positive,
But
Be honest
About the bad,

Because
I
Never want to
See
My friend sad,

I'll speak positively
Into their life
Because
I want
To see
Them
Rise,

A wise man
Never said
That
Your friends
Are family,
But
They are family
If they're
Not the enemy.

Too Late

Too late
There she goes
Over there

With that man

Just understand
You.
Weren't the one,

You were one step behind,
Lied numerous times
You were
Never a DIME,

But you took a PIECE
Of her
Energy

Didn't make her
Bride-to-be,

But
He
Took the cake

And fed it to her
Amongst friends

And you stand outside
The church
Hurt,

Because you burned
A heart
That healed
And killed yours

Kind of hard to ignore
That you,
Messed up

As you weep
Outside.
For what you
Denied

God
Holds karma
And He
Places it on you,

What you do
Has a reaction,
But
You weren't expecting

That.

A wagon
White gold
Diamond ring

You thought you were the prize,
But

Who has the ring?

Everything you've done

It doesn't mean
A thing
Now

She is
The queen,

And
You gave her nothing,
But
He gave
Her everything

All you can say is,
"Can I see the ring?"

I Didn't Make the Deadline

I didn't make the deadline,
But
I got an A

I wanted to graduate
Before '08

I studied for the test,
I brought my books,

But I
Never took
The degree,

I was one step away,
But they
Said
I must pay

So I walked away
To
Reevaluate,

Along my way,
I came across
What the Lord
Wanted me to find

He designed,

Me to feed
The people,
Not
The wallet,
With knowledge,

You got it

He said
You can be
What you tried
To pay for
And I could not ignore
Those words.

So I
Turned the tables,
Tossed

Them in the air
And watched them fall,

I got back up
Before I could crawl,
Because He told me to
Be obedient,

And
With God,
What can't you do?

It's true
I never agreed
With the way
They
Explained knowledge,

I got
The real
Version
And your
School got the off brand
Understand
You're just paying
More,
For less,

But I guess you can't
Be a doctor without
A degree
How you gone make
Money, honey?

You better go
To school
To save lives

Because our purpose
Is not the same.

No One Will

No one will
Alter my feelings,
No one can change
My mind

No one can decide
What's mine,

I'm
Self-made
Overly brave,

Can't be made
A fool of

I'm above
The negativity,
And beyond
The truth

I can't lose
My confidence
I can't lose
My God,
I am strong
On the inside,

I drive
To my destination
And pick up
Wisdom

I married him
And now
Live with him,

I send him
To the store
To pick up
Determination,

Now I'm
Waiting
For success
To come

I've won
Before winner

Loser ran
When I came

Because
He knew I gained
What I claimed

I have a name
That only God knows,
It's
Enclosed
In his book,

Because He took
Me
To new heights,
And
I was willing to
Climb

To find
My calling

I'm walking,
But I crawled
First

And fell
Three times
To learn
My lesson

Now I'm resting easy,

Believe me,
It was much harder
Than
You think,

But I was not
Designed
Weak

I pushed wrong
And embraced
Right

I fly so high
Because I am...

You're Moving

You're moving
Like a boat in the sea,
But
Away from me,

The conversations are minimum,
Our outings
Have faded

Someone's erasing
What we made

And
It hurts,

But

It was worth
The season
For a good reason:
You're leaving

You chose happiness
And
I can't be mad,
That your glad
In another time
Zone,

I zoned
Out
When you expressed
Your plans,
But
I had to be a fan
And understand
That you were leaving
The scene
To sing a
New song

Where you belong
We long for change
And you
Made that
Jump

And I have to adjust,

But this won't affect
What was left behind

We will shine in the sky as friends
You and I,

Are
Soul Queens
And we
Believe in loyalty

Forever in a day
I pray
That you stay
Positive and strong
Wherever you belong

Songs will play
Memories will grow
And I will show
Up at
Yo doh'
In
Yo
Time zone

Soul sister.

The Blind Can See Your Envy

The blind can see your envy,
The death can hear your remarks

Einstein
You're
Trying to out-smart,

You're
Far into the woods,
So gone that
You're lost,

You want to
Tear down
People
At any cost,

You lost
Trying to keep up
You didn't run
Your race

You run a fourteen,
But
Trying to keep up with Usain

You claim
The Lord,
But act against

You went
And spent
All your cents

You're driving down
My direction
Is up

You run around
Trying
To cause
A fuss,

You look. With envy
When you can get it
Too

What's going on

From me
To you,

I proved I cared,
Tried to
Take you high,

But you looked at
Me
With looks
Of hate,

I see
your face
I see
Your heart
And the way it's looking
Is very dark,

So far you're
Gone
In the wrong
Direction
And still,
You expect to get your blessing

That is a question.

My Words

My words,
They sink
Into you,

You hold them,
So tight
That I want,
To forget
I spoke

I hope
You forgive me,

I can't see,
The words
You choose
To hang on to

So I lose
You
Before,
I could gain,

It's so hard to say,
If you care,

But,

I am aware
Of my wrongs

So
I sing you songs,

That mean
Nothing

Which is haunting,
Me,

Because I spoke,
Death in depth,
And
I slept alone,

For so long,
You choose,
To keep my word

So my feelings hurt
And so does my
Heart
Because I never
Wanted to be apart
It's hard
To leave you,
When I'm the blame

I have stained
Your love,
With words
That are poison

Now I'm wanting
To remove the stain,
But
The pain
Overpowers,
The harder I try,
So I,
Pray,
To God,
That He forgives
My lies
When I tried,
To hurt you
Inside.

First Look and Find

First look and find,
What you're missin',
Before you add others,
To your mission,

You're missin',
The blessin',
Because,
You're guessin',
Who cares,

When it shouldn't matter,

Gather,
Information,
From our God,
Then,
Look inside,

Of your soul,
And gain control,
Of you,

Then you can understand
What can be done,
For ...them

Lift,
Up your hands
And stand,
With your head high
And you will
Feel
The Lord's presence

And you
Wouldn't be guessin'
Who cares,

It's far
To want love,
But
Love
You because
The Lord do,

There is proof,
But

You must
Have
Faith

It takes
Strength,
Wisdom,
Power, and courage,
But
You must not
Be
Discouraged,

Flourish in the Lord
And do His will
And you will
See the power in Him.

Who Can See The Wind?

Who can see the wind?
Who can touch the stars?
Who can travel far,
Without planes or cars?
Who can feel my thoughts?
Who can touch my hand?
Who can?
Not an average man,
I stand with you,
But only some can see,
That you are within me,
I see the Game of Life,
And I'll play by your rules,
Because,
All will see,
Who's the King,
Of every country,
Our sea is Your puddle,
Our world is Yours,
I can't ignore,
The truth,
Some, they look for proof,
But why need it?
When you feed it,
Every day,
Opening your eyes,
After you pray,
And you will say the same,
If you know the power of faith,
No man can take a life,
And say,
It's over,
He just put you,
In the hands
Of not an,
Average man.

So He Said

So he said,
He'd take your hand,
And show you the way,

He said so,
And did,
So,
Just one day,

He'd tell you secrets,
That are only for you,

You thought so,
And went off,

What he,
Told you,

He made you smile,
By saying sweet words,

Words so sweet,
They ran
So deep,
You couldn't see,

Any movement

He did not prove

What was expressed,

The rest
Of his words continued to flow,
And go,

In his direction,
Now it's affecting you,

Who,
Trusted
Broken promises,
So
Angry at yourself
Because you trusted
Words that you have not felt,
You dealt,

With it
For so long
Now you feel
His words
Target
Your
Intelligence

Pressing your mind with lies
Altering your emotions
Controlling
Your reaction
Your relationship
Is crashing,
Because you trusted words
And not action

Now you're
Acting,
Out of line
Because he
Spoke a good game,
And spoke
Sweet lies.

Pray

It's the sweetest memories that make me cry,
Because when you vanished,
It's that moment that,
I,
Want to speak and
Hear you reply,
My mind suddenly becomes logical,
When your body is no longer functioning,
I want your flesh
To stand next
To me,
But,
All I see
Is a world without thee?
It's unsettling,
To settle,
For more days without you,
But someone in the afterlife has a bigger
Vision for me, and (you)
Were my lessons, my friend?
Plus more,
You were you,
How could I ever ask for more?
And more memories of you cross my mind,
But when I match our memories to your face,
Tears fall,
My heart races,
And my face displays,
Happiness with a hint of pain,
I sing you a song
At random times,
It brings joy to my heart,
But tears in my eyes,
It's a struggle,
Day after day,
Wondering if the pain of
Missing you will ever go away,
I say,
I think I can,
I think I can,
And
Over time the memoirs will stay,
And God will show me the big plan that I can't see today,
So I pray.

Touch the Stars

Feed me knowledge,
It will,
Bring me food,
Knowing the unknown,
Will unlock the truth,
Sit and think,
Let's meditate,
Love to think,
Could be all it takes,
Surround yourself,
With,
What you dream,
Dreams are closer,
Than they seem,
Empty your mind,
To the world,
Come back refreshed
Boys and girls,

You're the future,
That's what you are,
Teach to act,
Let's touch the stars

www.ingramcontent.com/pod-product-compliance
Lightning Source LLC
Chambersburg PA
CBHW050641160426
43194CB00010B/1766